You don't have to be an athlete to know that good coaching makes all the difference in sports. In this life, we each have a unique race marked out for us, yet there are many hurdles to overcome. Nicole is the very best coach. She's vulnerable, humorously sharing her own stories of overcoming. It's incredible to consider all she accomplishes in this book: stirring you out of complacency, holding you accountable in love, motivating you to go further than you could imagine, and believing that you are a champion. While reading, I stopped many times and just lifted my hands—or closed my eyes in reflection. There was a lot of "Yes, Sis" happening, too!

We are created to flourish. If flourishing is what you seek, then savor these pages. Take time to reflect, to allow God's Spirit to guide you. And then go run your race fueled with God's power. Nicole has gifted us with words fitly spoken, inviting us to live up to the freedom Christ has achieved for us. Let's go, sisters!

DORENA WILLIAMSON, bestselling author and speaker

Courage and Confidence is an impactful work. . . . The intricate introduction of the concept of the created self versus the curated self describes the blueprint of God's intended plan for our purpose. . . . Reading this incredible activation piece has shifted a gear in this current season for me—a clarion call that this book is God's investment.

YOLANDA D. MERCER, author of *Born to Be Wild*

Courage and Confidence is a practical guide to help the everyday woman launch forward in her calling! It engages universal questions such as *Who am I?* and *Why am I here?* while also addressing *How do I get from where I am today to where I want to be?* Nicole's candor in storytelling, transparency of the truth, and ideological reframing helps us unbox the things we tend to hold on to for far too long. It's a contagious read—you just want to keep reading! You will laugh, you may even cry, but it will help you connect faith to your fear, hope to your despair, and victory to your vulnerability. Hold on to those outlined Scriptures, keep journaling through those prompts, and be prepared to unbox the best version of you!

PASTORS COLVIN AND **MONIQUE CHAMBERS,**
EKM Toronto Church

Nicole is the friend and coach you want in your corner, equipping you with the right tools and fighting alongside you to live according to your God-given purpose. Her personality and confidence shine on every page—she walks the walk of this message and is passionate about helping others live it out too. You'll return to this book again and again in seasons where you find yourself getting in your own way. So many of her words stopped me in my tracks, and I found myself thinking, *Oh, that's GOOD*.

JENN SCHULTZ, author of *She's Not Your Enemy*

In a world often clouded by self-doubt and limited thinking, *Courage and Confidence* stands out as a guiding light, illuminating the path toward boldly discovering your God-given purpose. This remarkable book seamlessly blends Nicole's extensive coaching experience with deep spiritual insights to guide readers on a transformative journey of self-discovery, growth, and faith.

As someone who has had the privilege of witnessing Nicole empower and uplift countless lives through her coaching and speaking, I can confidently say that this book is a testament to her burning passion to help others find their purpose and live a life unboxed to step into all that God has for them. She has masterfully condensed her years of wisdom and practical expertise into these pages, making it a treasure box for anyone looking to deepen their relationship with God and maintain a confident and purpose-filled life.

Courage and Confidence is a one-of-a-kind book that will leave a lasting impact on your life. It's not just a read; it's an experience that will help you unbox your potential and ignite your heart to step fully into becoming the person God has called you to be. Nicole's book is a beacon of hope for those who seek to conquer their insecurities, detox themselves of limited thinking, find their inner strength, and embrace their authenticity.

It's a must-read for anyone looking to step outside the box of the mundane life.

CHERYL NEMBHARD, author, speaker, TV host of *See, Hear, Love,* and podcast host of *On the Path with Cheryl Nembhard*

Anyone willing to start the conversation about daughters of God unapologetically stepping into their Kingdom assignment has caught my attention. But Nicole Salmon, inciting within readers a violent uprising against years of misconstrued beliefs, traumatic experiences, and deceptive inner dialogues, made *Courage and Confidence* an even more delightful read. Make picking up this book your declaration to not be less than you were purposed to be.

PASTOR SHARO RAMKHELAWAN, senior pastor of HopeNYC Church and founder of Preacher Girl TV

The difficult truth is we are often our own barrier when it comes to embracing our purpose. We may settle for living life as our curated self instead of the woman God created us to be. In *Courage and Confidence*, Nicole O. Salmon doesn't just write from her years of experience coaching women; she vulnerably shares how she learned to embrace her God-given purpose despite her own barriers. This book is real, encouraging, practical, and written with the gentle push you need to come out of hiding. It is a transparent, gospel-filled guide that has been crafted with the tender heart of a woman in mind. Nicole has earned her title as "The Purpose Coach," and whether you are actively living out your purpose or just starting to explore what your purpose is, I am confident she will help you unbox the woman you were always meant to be.

KIA STEPHENS, author, speaker, and founder of Entrusted Women

NICOLE O. SALMON

Courage and Confidence

A Bold Guide to Unboxing Who You Were Created to Be

A NavPress resource published in alliance with Tyndale House Publishers

NavPress.com

Courage and Confidence: A Bold Guide to Unboxing Who You Were Created to Be

A NavPress resource published in alliance with Tyndale House Publishers

The Team:

David Zimmerman, Publisher; Deborah Sáenz Gonzalez, Acquisitions Editor; Elizabeth Schroll, Copyeditor; Jennifer Phelps, Designer

Author is represented by the literary agency of Embolden Media Group, www.emboldenmediagroup.com.

For information about special discounts for bulk purchases, please contact Tyndale House Publishers at csresponse@tyndale.com, or call 1-855-277-9400.

ISBN 978-1-64158-833-1

Printed in the United States of America

30 29 28 27 26 25 24
7 6 5 4 3 2 1

To you, dear reader,

for having the courage
and confidence to trust
what God is revealing to
you and to boldly chart
your own course.

Your destiny was worth
the crush, discipline, and
victories that were required
to write this book.

Contents

Introduction

Unboxing Your Created Self

There is a score you must learn how to settle because it is one you will have to face with each new season of life. As insightful as you are, you still have moments when you ask yourself, *Who am I, and what has God created me to do?* Even in your greatest moments of clarity, you still desire reassurance. You are searching for the permission to allow yourself to trust what God is revealing to you and to chart your own course.

The score you must learn how to settle is between your *created* self and your *curated* self.

The created self is the nature God designed and shaped each of us in. It is an untainted reflection of His image, accented with all the unique elements of our individual temperaments, abilities, and gifts. It is contoured with truth and anchored in the written and spoken word of God. But you don't always feel anchored. As you negotiate aspects of your created self, you long to be confident, clear, consistent, and resolute about the woman you were created to be.

Picking up this book is your declaration. It is you settling the score that you will no longer deny, discount, disregard, diminish, or defer your created self to let the counterfeit known as your curated self take center stage. The curated self is the nature we adopt from social and familial influences, then adapt as needed. When we live from the curated self rather than living as an expression of our Creator, we become an expression of what we have designed, who life and circumstances have shaped us into being, all while shrouding our God-given design. If you truly want the image of God to win so you can experience the freeness and fruitfulness of a purpose-filled life, then you must be willing to yield completely to the unapologetic process of unboxing your created self.

Sunday sermons alone are no longer enough for you. Your appetite has been awakened. You desire to sink your teeth into content that is meaty, and you want to be challenged. You want more. You have a lot of questions, and everything about the season you are in feels unconventional. You've developed a slight disdain for what you once loved. What used to excite you is now draining you, and what you once felt called to now feels like an unsettling compromise. You have a deep longing for safe spaces where you can pour out your frustrations on empathetic ears and not be met with blank stares as though you have just shared something blasphemous or profane.

You've been sensing a level of righteous unrest, and it will not let you continue to be the same woman, in the same place, living out half your potential on a quarter of your anointing. It's time for a supernatural release. As a fellow sojourner, I have to be completely transparent with you: It's going to get uncomfortable. I love you too much to lie to you, and I am speaking to you with a heavenly boldness and an urgency that has no room for fluff. This book is coming for your heart like an arrow in the hands of a skilled archer because it's time for your harvest.

Through the guidance of Holy Spirit, I have thoughtfully included prayers, Scriptures, exercises, prophetic declarations, journal prompts, transparent and vulnerable personal stories, and a number of application features to encourage and aid you in looking inward and applying the unboxing prompts as you are reading. I encourage you to keep a designated journal for your unboxing reflections and insights.

Allow Holy Spirit to unbox you on these pages. Allow Him to meet you between the lines and give you the clarity, release, and room to show up fully and consistently in your life. Your family, friends, and colleagues as well as the saints and the ain'ts will probably think you have lost your home training when you start making the kinds of freeing faith moves I share in this book about unboxing and coming into alignment with your created self. If you were never given room to question, ponder, or carve a path of your own, unboxing your created self may lead you into moments of wondering if you've done something sinful, unbiblical, or just plain wrong. Taking the lid off your potential will do that to you.

Your shift toward a more purpose-led and purpose-aligned life may unsettle many around you, and you might start to feel like you've crossed a line. But you have actually been a squatter, occupying spaces that were meant to only be seasons and calling them your home.

Evict her, I hear in my spirit. I have been commissioned to deliver notice that it is your time to both go and grow.

In this book you will pick up the tools you need to unleash the courage to evict yourself from your curated comforts and stand confidently in your created identity. Let me help you

- reclaim your voice and become reacquainted with the voice of Holy Spirit so you can become more decisive and save more time;
- interrupt the cycle of second-guessing who you are so you can operate more confidently in your purpose and see your dreams realized;
- stop determining your progress by the obstacles you are facing so you can create more consistency in your life and see your goals through to completion; and
- replace old thought patterns and habits that produce inaction with a thought life that leads to overcoming guilt and condemnation and achieving more results.

You cannot stay where you are any longer. Not one more day. Your true home—the version of yourself that has been divinely inspired and wired—cannot be filled by anyone but you. You have not missed your chance. And even though many of the things declared about you seem delayed, they are still yours for the taking if you are ready and willing to make a courageous move toward the life of purpose you were *created* for.

1
The Need to Unbox
Unboxing the Fall That Started It All

Identity apart from divinity
is always going to be hollow.
MARSHAWN EVANS DANIELS

You can recognize a woman who has been unboxed. This kind of woman is confident, decisive, and clear about her purpose. She knows how to confidently and gracefully say no to anything that will divert her from her calling. She is fully aware of her assets, and most importantly, she knows how to use them. She takes pleasure in mastering and staying in her lane. This woman shines whether she's in the role of a CEO or a barista. Her work does not define her understanding of her value. She is full and content. She is also patient and kind with herself, fully accepting of God's grace for her very human shortcomings. God is her King, and she knows this unequivocally. And while not everyone she encounters can pinpoint God as her divine source of courage, they can certainly sense it. After all, as a carrier of God's glory, she produces much fruit in her life.

This is a picture of our created self. It is the nature God designed and shaped us in. An untainted reflection of His image, accented with all the unique elements of our temperament, abilities, and gifts. It is contoured with truth and anchored in the written and spoken word of God.

The fall of humanity interrupted that construct and the expression of this created self. When Adam and Eve disobeyed God in the Garden of Eden, they covered their nakedness and hid (Genesis 3:6-8). Before this, there was never any shame or questioning of their uncovered form. It was beautiful. It was good. The introduction of sin, however, brought with it an identity crisis. Adam and Eve's disobedience (sin) separated them from God, the source and standard of their goodness. The separation left them feeling vulnerable and exposed, and under this perceived pressure, they scrambled to try to regain that blissful *good*ness on their own. Adam and Eve proceed to make coverings for themselves by sewing together fig leaves from their surroundings. This clearly was not *good* enough to hide their newly developed fears and insecurities. We know this because when God comes looking for them, He finds them hiding.

> They heard the sound of the LORD God walking in the garden in the cool of the day, and the man and his wife hid themselves from the presence of the LORD God among the trees of the garden. But the LORD God called to the man and said to him, "Where are you?" And he said, "I heard the sound of you in the garden, and I was afraid, because I was naked, and I hid myself."
>
> GENESIS 3:8-10

This Scripture stirs a few thoughts for me:

1. No hiding place is so distant or fortified that we cannot hear the Lord.
2. We can use the very things God gave us as hiding places.
3. When God calls us out of hiding, it causes us to address what drove us to that place, admit the effect it had on us, and confess that we are not where we are supposed to be.

God allowed Adam and Eve to have their own unboxing experience in the Garden.

The Godlike creatures who had always shared in fellowship with God and each other, just as they were, were experiencing the compounding consequences of sin. They went from the uninhibited freedom of living from their created selves to feeling like they could not stand in the presence of God (or anyone else, for that matter) because on their own, they were no longer "good enough."

The effect of the Fall on our identity may look different for us than it did for Adam and Eve, but the outcome is still the same: hiding.

This new, less glorious image of who we really are is what I call our curated self. It is a distorted mash-up of everything our parents and other authority figures got wrong, highlighted by many of the things they got right. Though desirous of God's will, the curated self is enslaved to the rigor of trying to please its way into being accepted by others. This self is dented by misguided words and directives said with good intentions by people who have never been unboxed themselves but who thought they knew what was best for us. The curated self is brimming with misapplied abilities anxiously waiting to be reclaimed, mentored, and aligned with biblical truth.

Therein lies the challenge. Will you own your created identity, or will you forfeit to your curated self? If you truly want the image of God to win, then you must submit yourself to the process of unboxing. Here is why. This dilemma between our curated and created selves leads to the unsettling junction between dissatisfaction and contentment, between *This place is not good enough* and *I am fine where I am.* I have found myself there on many occasions, purchased real estate, and set up shop. I could feel the desperation and hear the quiet whimper of my suffocating created self.

I had a body count of relationships that met my superficial needs but not my supernatural destiny. The men I dated weren't marriage material, and to make matters worse, we weren't spiritually aligned. Each relationship, the next worse than the last, was with a man I had to keep hidden from those who knew my created self so they wouldn't see—after a close-up look—that my good life was actually a hoax. I also had to keep my created self a secret from the men I dated, to hold on to my little piece of fool's gold. I couldn't want too much, share too deeply, or reveal the breadth of my capabilities. Sir, I actually know how to jump-start a car, strip a faulty wire and get it working again, and troubleshoot the most complex problems. I was capable of more, but being able to check the "taken" box was important to feeling good about myself, so I kept my little secret. It felt good and gross at the same time. It was years before I learned that if the shoe didn't fit, I could change it instead of pretending it wasn't hurting, mashing, and bruising me. My inaction, apathy, and poor choices buried my created self alive, and now my curated "good" would have to be good enough. At least so I thought. The problem is, conceding to a subpar version of your created self requires you to suppress your greatness for the perceived ease of a life that in reality detains you. Others might describe such a life as good, but you can't shake the feeling that you are betraying God and yourself.

I am stirred to another thought. A fond memory, actually. Being satisfied with a knock-off version of who we are reminds me of my experience of drifting down the lazy river at the water park I loved visiting as a kid. No paddling or breast strokes were required to enjoy this classic attraction. You simply lay on a giant inflatable donut and let the gentle current take you on a scenic tour around the park. The water was never more than chest deep on my four-foot frame, and no one was allowed to splash or make waves lest it disturb the bliss of the other people barely floating along. It was very relaxing under the warm sun. But I am an advanced-stroke-level swimmer, and I had come to swim! There was no room within the narrow current to do what I loved and did so well. The lazy river was always enjoyable, but my parents had not paid the hefty entrance fee for me to lie on a floaty and drift in circles all day. At some point I had to make my way to the main attraction: the beach-like replica called the wave pool.

Much like the lazy river, your life may be very enjoyable. Not much effort is required to keep things moving moderately along. And perhaps a life of drifting gives you peace, and your joy is complete. If this is true, then drift on. But friend, God did not pay the hefty price of sending His only Son to a gory and undeserved death for you and me to lie there and drift. Nothing spectacular that would make the world gaze in awe and see Jesus in us can come from a suppressed life when we were clearly fashioned to do so much more. Drifting is another way that we hide. I suppose Adam and Eve could have just as easily been in a marsh under a stack of pussy willows. We can get really creative when we want to camouflage our disobedience.

Walking in the power of your created self will result in making waves and disturbing those around you who are perfectly content with their drifting. Perhaps they are fulfilling their highest calling. Perhaps that thing we call purpose rests peacefully within them as they obediently float by. But as early as I can remember, before my *goo-goo*s became *ga-ga*s, I had an unbridled desire to speak and creatively express myself. As I grew older, I didn't coincidentally become a preacher, a coach, and an author. The capacity for all those roles was always within me, splashing around and making it nearly impossible to drift.

I am certain you, too, have some early memories of self expression, times when you felt in your element. Those memories hold intel about your created self and have left breadcrumbs that led you to some of your current roles or aspirations. More importantly, they point to the natural abilities and spiritual gifts that give you the capability to approach certain experiences with ease, fulfillment, and distinction. Your created identity has always been giving you prompts. It is not always found in your big achievements but in the attributes you may be overlooking. You are still not convinced that who you are is not found in what you do but in the uniqueness of how you see and approach everything you do. As you look back and connect those early promptings to what you are sensing and learning about yourself now, you kinda-sorta-maybe-probably knew all along that drifting is not for you.

If you are in the company of drifters, they may have

convinced you that you should be satisfied, even happy, with how long you have been able to keep afloat. I know too well the strain of meeting all the outward markers of happiness while feeling hollow at the same time. It is a gaping hole that only you and God can see while others applaud you for doing a good job. "Happy" and hollow is what you feel when you have stayed in a great job for too long, have stopped at attaining a diploma when God told you to get the degree, and have chosen Mr. Good Enough because the loneliness of waiting for Mr. Good was unbearable. "Happy" and hollow is that sinking feeling in the pit of your stomach or the heavy weight you feel on your chest when you are celebrated for an accomplishment that was never God's desire for you. "Happy" and hollow is the torturous tug-of-war between living in your curated self rather than your created self. Before you know it, you start to call these types of compromises destiny when it really is drifting.

As if this woe wasn't enough, there is also a deception older than time that "good enough" is easier than the painfully rewarding fulfillment of pursuing, pressing into, and producing greatness—the fulfillment of all the Godlike attributes you were *created* to employ. You could continue to ignore the restlessness of leading a misaligned life, but greatness suppressed only produces pressure. And while there is a popular saying that "pressure makes diamonds," another wise adage recommends caution: "Pressure bursts pipes."

The Unboxed Experience

This brings us to another predicament you may be facing: trying to contain what needs to be unboxed.

As we look to the Scriptures, we find Moses, who was born at a dangerous and inconvenient time in the history of the Israelites. Pharaoh ordered the midwives to kill all the baby boys born to the Israelites. Like a true nurturer, Moses' mother hid her new son out of necessity. It was only a matter of time before her efforts to protect him could no longer conceal him.

> The woman conceived and bore a son, and when she saw that he was a fine child, she hid him three months. **When she could hide him no longer**, she took for him a basket made of bulrushes and daubed it with bitumen and pitch. She put the child in it and placed it among the reeds by the river bank.
>
> EXODUS 2:2-3, EMPHASIS ADDED

Moses' mother hid him among the reeds of the riverbank. Adam and Eve hid among the trees of the Garden. And you, my sister, where have you been hiding?

It may be premature, but I would like to give you your first unboxing task by asking you to write down all the places you have been hiding. What are your trees and reeds? Here are some intentional and unintentional coverings you may have made for yourself.

work	child(ren)
titles	spouse
possessions	singleness
family	friends
sickness	pride
tradition	humility
physical appearance	talent
wit	humor
unforgiveness	

Write down the ones that are applicable to you, including any that are not on this list, on a separate sheet of paper. Place your list somewhere private but visible enough to keep you accountable to addressing and avoiding these coverings as you do the work required to live out your created identity.

I see you, woman of God. And please don't be mistaken. Those who haven't openly affirmed you see you too. You couldn't box up your confidence and hide it, even though you've tried. Like baby Moses, perhaps hiding for a season had its place, but you, too, have been growing. You have been challenging the status quo, asking the hard questions, pushing your personal limits, and who you were truly created to be can no longer be hidden.

In his introduction to the art exhibit "In Plain Sight," executive director of Berkeley Art Center Daniel Nevers writes, "The paradox of the visible remaining unperceived is a function of our need to filter sensory information in order to navigate the world."[1] So then, what we have seen, heard, and even lived must be unboxed so we can expose that which was missed and misunderstood as we've hurried about life as we've known it.

You could continue hiding among the trees of the Garden or the reeds of the riverbank, but picking up this book is your declaration. It is you settling the score that you will no longer deny, discount, disregard, diminish, or defer your created self to let the counterfeit known as your curated self take center stage. If you truly want the image of God to win so you can experience the freeness and fruitfulness of a purpose-filled life, then you must be willing to yield completely to the unapologetic process of unboxing your created self.

Let the Unboxing Begin

God wants you to be free from the burden of trying to be good enough. Unboxing is where you declutter your perspective of yourself and activate your courage and confidence in Christ. It is how you create the shift necessary to get unstuck and illuminate what needs to be evaluated, elevated, or eliminated.

Discerning What Needs to Be Evaluated

Should I keep doing this? Determining what should stay or go in your life requires the objectivity of Holy Spirit to examine, unpack, and detangle the beliefs, relationships, and experiences that have shaped and nurtured your understanding of purpose and your created self. It is an ongoing process of separating the junk from the gems.

Pausing to undergo this type of personal inventory is self-rediscovery at its finest. Self-discovery 2.0. Deep diving, divulging, and debunking everything you've been taught or caught about your identity and purpose that is not true, biblical, or serving you well. Liberation from the holding patterns you may have curated or that were handed to you that keep you stuck, unsure, and questioning your created capabilities.

This is how you can live from a place of courage and confidence in the face of the cares, conversations, and social constructs of life that have the potential to blur, bury, and block your perception of who you are and what you are capable of through Jesus Christ. It is how you mitigate your inconsistencies and the tendency to vacillate between two versions of self.

Discerning What Needs to Be Elevated

This is where you become able to affirm *I need to keep doing this*. Elevating your internal and external assets involves bringing those assets to the forefront that brokenness, insecurity, or ignorance may have left behind. It requires the deliberate discipline of sitting with yourself long enough and regularly enough to be challenged and changed by Holy Spirit. This is a principal part of purpose-led living. Becoming radically clear is how we stabilize our thoughts and actions to align with who God has designed us to be so we can live more intentionally and obediently. You will need to habitually engage in the process of unboxing your created self and actively press toward the woman God not only created but also sent His Son to die for so that through His resurrection, you could be reconciled to Him and to your created self.

The apostle Paul wrote,

> Not that I have already obtained it [this goal of being Christlike] or have already been made perfect, but I actively press on so that I may take hold of that [perfection] for which Christ Jesus took hold of me *and* made me His own. Brothers and sisters, I do not consider that I have made it my own yet; but one thing *I do*: forgetting what *lies* behind and reaching forward to what *lies* ahead, I press on toward the goal to win the [heavenly] prize of the upward call of God in Christ Jesus. All of us who are mature [pursuing spiritual perfection] should have this attitude. And if in any respect you have a different attitude, that too God will make clear to you. Only let us stay true to what we have already attained.[2]
>
> PHILIPPIANS 3:12-16, AMP

Discerning What Needs to Be Eliminated

Aka *I need to get rid of this.* This kind of unboxing is not bound to a set schedule. You already know what the prompting feels like. If you are not determining what you should eliminate, you probably have already experienced yourself forgetting, forfeiting, and frustrating your purpose and asking the same old questions. Perhaps they are familiar: *Why am I here? What is my purpose? Can I do this?* and *Am I good enough?* Not unboxing is why so many fall over and over into the same unsatisfying slump and stay there—never activating or actualizing their potential and succumbing to depression, apathy, emptiness, confusion, a lack of motivation, and inaction.

Any interaction or information that leaves you feeling icky about yourself or causes your pre-Christ nature to rise up has to go.

Chapter Check-In

No hiding place is so distant or fortified that you cannot hear the Lord. I would like you to pause and consider how God has been speaking to you. What has He been saying about your identity?

Journal Prompt: God is calling me out of hiding, and I admit that these are the things that drove me there . . .

Remember: Picking up this book is your declaration. It is you settling the score that you will no longer deny, discount, disregard, diminish, or defer your created self to let the counterfeit known as your curated self take center stage.

2
The Box You Were Given
Unboxing Your Belief System

Every crisis creates unexpected problems. Every crisis also creates unprecedented opportunities. The best leaders address the problems and seize the opportunities!
CRAIG GROESCHEL

When we were little, the adults around us were often trying to hide things from us—"big-people business," my parents would call it—grown-up details shared over whispered phone calls and conversations moved to more private rooms so they would not be heard. But what they failed to realize is that many of the things the adults in our lives tried their best to keep us from hearing or seeing we still heard and saw. These conversations and experiences, like many of the others we would soon absorb on our way to adulthood, were shaping us.

If we are going to have a fighting chance at living a purpose-filled life, we must begin reflecting on and unpacking the encrypted messages we've observed throughout our life—the messages that have shaped our curated self and the box many of us find ourselves living in. More specifically, I want us to drill down and allow Holy Spirit to awaken the subconscious teleprompter that feeds us lines and shapes our construct of purpose, function, and identity.

I am not asking for an exhaustive list of all the encrypted messages you've encountered. You don't need one. We are deep diving for those messages frozen in time that, without even knowing it, we have hung our reality on and called it truth.

If These Walls Could Talk

I giggle to myself at times because I can still hear my mother's voice telling me what to do. I'm grown! I can hear her telling me to sit up when I am slouching at my desk. I hear "Lean up off the counter" as I am washing the dishes and the front of my shirt is getting sopping wet. Words cling to the soul. They form memories and don't always go "in one ear and out the other," as the saying proposes. Some words have a way of resurfacing and locating you years after they have left the lips of the messenger. They find their way into your thoughts, emotions, perspective, and identity, speaking not only to you but for you.

Almost twenty years ago, I overheard a conversation, and I can repeat it word for word all these years later. I was at work during their busy season, and around noon I anticipated that I wasn't going to be able to sign off and run out the door at quitting time, as was my usual practice. I had a responsibility to support the extra workload that came annually during their peak season, but it wasn't my priority. My priority was to get into my car and, after weaving down backstreets, pick up my son from the babysitter on time. Asking me to leave even five minutes later than usual didn't seem like a big ask to my employer, but for a single mother who had not secured permanent childcare arrangements and was at the mercy of a time-conscious babysitter, five minutes meant I was going to be late. And if I was late, I would need to find other childcare arrangements. And you guessed it: I had no other arrangements.

My familial atmosphere was a very small bubble. I knew I had at least two-and-a-half trusted sources I could turn to for help, but I took great pride in being a self-reliant, uber independent single mother who took care of her responsibilities. But that day, I needed help! I let my guard down and turned to my village for support. I made an SOS call from the company phone that hung on the wall in a narrow, quiet hallway outside the break room. "Hello," I whispered as I made my appeal to my trusted familial support. They were nearby and gladly agreed to pick up my son and run an errand or two with him onboard to provide the extra thirty minutes of childcare I desperately needed.

"Hello," I said again, this time slightly shouting with my mouth pressed to the receiver. "I forgot an important detail," I said all breathy and loud. They needed to know the safe word in order for the babysitter to release my son into their care.

I could still hear them rustling around because they had not successfully disconnected the call. I realized my trusted help was in a noisy public salon. Those within earshot of our call asked them if everything was okay. They went on to explain my dilemma. "Where is the child's father?" a nosy bystander inquired of them. And then it happened. Words! They went in one ear and did not go out the other. Hot, salty tears streamed down my face as I listened to their casual reply: "I don't know where the father is." They continued, "You know these young people. They have babies and then they can't take care of them."

Jesus take the wheel! This couldn't be happening. Why on earth would this two-faced heathen double-cross me, causing public shame? This was someone I trusted. This was someone who knew what a responsible parent I was. This was someone who knew my son's father was also at work and couldn't get there in time even if he tried.

I was so visibly overwhelmed with grief that day the company sent me home early in a taxicab. They couldn't risk the liability of an accident because I was driving distracted while tears and emotions blurred my vision of the road.

Almost twenty years have passed, and I can still remember the words that were said that day. The most painful part is that I remember how those words made me feel (betrayed).

Those words became feelings (distrust). Those feelings became a message I started to live my life by: *Do not ask for help because it will be thrown in your face.*

My trusted help and I have reconciled since that day. It was the healthy, biblical thing to do, and it took time. But that message became an emotional stronghold that would affect my ability to allow others to help me, even to the detriment of my physical and mental health, and I'm still unboxing it. Take a second to highlight the word *still,* because you need to know that I am not pitching you an unsustainable, quick-fix life hack. Every unboxing principle in this book requires unboxing over time.

What have you heard that is now speaking for you? Conversations and indirect messages that have resurfaced and interject *No*, *Can't*, *Won't*, or *Not possible* before you can even process what is happening and make a sound decision for yourself. It's time to reclaim your voice and become reacquainted with the voice of Holy Spirit. In chapter 6, we will discuss some cognitive and spiritual strategies for mindset mastery. Until then, let's continue and unpack a few binding belief systems that war against the survival of our created self.

Binding Belief Systems

1. Perfection Is the Standard We Must Uphold

Olivia was raised by a father who felt like he had a lot to prove to the world. After a failed marriage, he was determined Olivia would be the proof and validation he needed to affirm that though his marriage had declined, he knew how to get something right. Olivia was only nine years old when her mother left, and her father's need for Olivia to excel and get things right was a burden she could feel. It didn't leave much room for her to grow through the natural process of getting some things wrong. Coloring pages had to be completed without going outside the lines. An A or 99 percent on a test was not enough without the plus or 100 percent. By the time Olivia made it to university, she had developed so much performance anxiety that her grades started to slip, and she was placed on academic probation. When her father and friends would check in, she covered up the decline of her grades and mental health. Olivia couldn't bear the thought of being yet another relationship her father wasn't good at. He had a bumper sticker, hat, hoodie, and mug with her school's logo so he wouldn't miss an opportunity to say "My daughter goes to school there" to anyone who might ask. Olivia's academic probation turned into getting expelled from school and losing her on-campus housing. After one too many missed phone calls, her father decided to drive up for a visit. He eventually tracked her down to the small windowless room that she was renting in town. For the first time, Olivia was met with compassion, warmth, and empathy from her father. His heart was broken when he learned that his daughter had allowed things to go this far because she felt that maintaining an image of perfection meant more to him than her well-being.

The indirect message of "only perfection allowed" lurks

in many classrooms, households, congregations, and boardrooms. The truth is, the world, our families, and our churches are full of imperfect people. That freeing truth is best articulated in John 8:32: "You will know the truth, and the truth will set you free." But at times that truth can also be ugly, messy, and require commitment to the long game for healing, transformation, and restoration to take place. Because this journey to freedom leads us through some uncomfortable places, many continue to live in the bondage of perfectionism that only deprives us of the progressive maturity described in the Epistles (1 Corinthians 13:11; Ephesians 4:13; Hebrews 6:1; 2 Peter 3:18). We have settled for looking good over the vulnerability of striving to be good.

Over the years, I have observed a whole culture of people choosing comfort over having hard conversations. Anyone can be a critic. Having mature love means being willing to step up and into the courage required to confront character inconsistencies. It means graciously guiding others toward behaviors and lifestyles that promote godly character and purpose-led living. Instead we often choose the convenience of "minding our own business" or looking the other way. It is much easier to talk *about* someone than to talk *to* them. What if they get mad, quit, walk away, push back, or cleave to denial? The evil of this kind of selfish silence is that it keeps us from the kind of accountability that might mean waiting a year or even longer while our talents and agendas sit on the sidelines so we can heal, rest, or receive the mentorship we need to mature and reach self-actualization. It may also involve losing money, relationships, promotions, or whatever shiny achievement makes us experience feelings of happiness and those we are accountable to look good. *Look good.* There it is again. It's the same predicament Adam and Eve found themselves in in the Garden. We have truly inherited their sin-born dilemma.

The messaging was incorrect but clear. It said, *Your mess is embarrassing and inconvenient. But as long as you play the part, we'll ignore your heart.* The misconstrued virtue of integrity paved the way for years of inconsistencies in my own character and many buried skeletons. I suppressed moral struggles that would go unshared and unshaken for decades as I replicated the modeled notion of *Don't ask, don't tell.* It curated in me perfectionism, the need to overachieve, and my inner critic—three deadly vices to living in the power of our created identity.

Trying to maintain an image of perfectionism will cause you to stay fixed on a task, job, or season beyond the grace God extended for it. The result is years of no fruit and unfulfillment. It is often rooted in rejection and an insatiable need for acceptance.

The overachiever sets a bar for themselves that God never asks for. This often results in a shocking blow to their confidence and courage when they discover that God is not pleased that they've prioritized their ego over their obedience.

So what does a holy God require? I imagine King David asked the same question and landed at this: "You will not delight in sacrifice, or I would give it; you will not be pleased with a burnt offering. The sacrifices of God are a broken spirit; a broken and contrite heart, O God, you will not despise" (Psalm 51:16-17).

Could a holy God be satisfied with the gift of our broken pieces placed on His altar? The answer is a resounding yes!

When we exegete the text, we find that the best thing Adam and Eve could have done on the day they hid in the Garden was to meet God like every other day, uncovered and humbled by their fall from grace instead of humiliated by it.

When you have spent formative years observing performance being prioritized over people actually dealing with their "stuff," true godly and loving accountability is replaced with an unwelcomed squatter called the inner critic. It sounds a lot like the loving rebuke and guidance you should have received but with a booming, destructive undertone of judgment, condemnation, negativity, and defeatism. Loving rebukes are painful and shameful to receive at times, but they are necessary to delicately divide who we are at our created core from the curated counterfeit that our sin, nature, and nurture has produced.

2. There Is No Room for Mistakes

In the last few years we've seen an uptick in the number of public figures who have been knocked from their pedestals for making a costly mistake—usually saying something wrong or acting in an inappropriate way. Patterns of abuse and gross misconduct should never be tolerated. However, honest mistakes that don't cause grave damage or harm should be stepping stones, not tombstones. I am not a fan of cancel culture, nor am I convinced that it is as good a means for keeping people accountable as it boasts.

Canceling usually unfolds in three phases. Someone makes a gross misstep, either in action or with their words. Next, they are hauled into social media's court of public opinion where complete strangers debate over the error of the offender's ways. Lastly, the verdict is rendered—canceled! The canceled individual loses their job, platform, or whatever seems fitting to the offense or will at least appease the roaring crowd.

Very few people bounce back from the ordeal of being canceled. Whether the verdict is warranted or premature, lives fade into obscurity at the hands of an equally flawed jury.

A similar dynamic is found at the root of our impatience with imperfection. It robs the world of some of God's best gifts. I've seen prodigies who were given up on because their genius was superseded by a series of poor life choices. Marriages prematurely dissolved because missteps led to mistrust that couldn't be forgiven. Thought leaders cut down before their ideas could reach maturation because of words spoken out of turn—words that, with guidance, could have evolved into the next social justice movement or Azusa Street Revival. In other words, they were canceled. Grace was treated like an old wives' tale. Though it should be a free gift, grace became something to be worked for, jumping through human-made hoops to get it.

You may be reading this from the margins just outside

the acceptance zone, somewhere from the nosebleed section of the game called life, sporting a jersey with a huge letter *D* on your chest for "Discarded." You know too well the sting of being canceled by others, canceled by yourself, or feeling canceled by God. On one hand, you do not ascribe to a version of grace that permits indecency as a way of life, calling it freedom in Christ. On the other hand, you do not have a standard of holiness that demands perfection while piously celebrating living an error-free life. It is within this tension that we must live daily. We are constantly doing the work and surrendering to God's work on our heart to make us more like Christ, a work that God is faithfully completing. Dwelling within either extreme is exhausting and depletes the measure of grace we can extend to our own personal failures and those of others.

Why is understanding the tension of grace so important to living a purpose-led life? Because the acceptance and application of grace means there is room for the process. We do not need to live in fear of missing out on a purpose-filled life. Second Timothy 1:7 reads: "God gave us a spirit **not of fear** but of power and love and self-control" (emphasis added).

Do you hear that? Instinctively we may not identify what we are feeling as fear, but what if we tackled 2 Timothy 1:7 a bit differently by starting at the end of the text and working our way back to the beginning? It's a little reverse engineering hack I do with myself when I feel disconnected from new truth or an unlived experience. Let's try it.

- Three of the many good gifts God gives us are power, love, and self-control.
- Over time, the unmanaged presence of fear in our lives results in the opposite of these three gifts remaining active.
- Instead, insecurity, intolerance, and a lack of discipline begin to materialize. (I selected a few antonyms to keep you on your toes.)

Insecurity. Intolerance. Lack of discipline. Have you noticed any of these strongholds in your life? If you answered yes, then it is time you evict fear and receive the power, love, and self-control (sobriety and sound judgment)[1] that have supernaturally been made available to you. Here is a prayer of declaration to relinquish fear's hold and receive God's many good gifts:

Dear God, I acknowledge that fear does not come from You. It has no place or legal authority in my life. I command it to go from my thought life and my lived life. I ask You to bind up and make whole the areas of brokenness it gained access through. I now put on love, power, and self-control. Help me trust Your process and Your pace as You perfect my purpose. In Jesus' name, amen.

3. Your Choices Are Final

Opening yourself up to the process (aka change) might be difficult if you are inherently holding on to the notion that your choices are final. For example: You chose to go to nursing school, but now there is a clash between your career and your calling. A final mindset says you are obligated to remain in that field even though the decision to stay is leading you further and further away from God's will.

I would like to propose that this false reality may not be fear based at all but a fixed idea that was formed in your early years by familial influences. I need you to think broader than just mother and father here. Think in terms of familial atmosphere. Somewhere in there lies the examples your parents were shaped by that have now become the hardwiring you live by.

We must look back a generation or two at the expectations our parents or familial influencers lived under because their ecosystems have influenced how we understand what *choice* is, a foundational concept to living a purpose-led life. When we look back a few generations to the false messages about choice our ancestors were exposed to at church, work, and home, we can see how they have made their way into our deepest patterns of thinking and may be at the root of our rigidity to allowing Holy Spirit to bend, shape, and course correct us into His purposes.

For many of our familial influencers, church membership came with an unspoken commitment code. They could only move on from their church with the endorsement of the community if they were relocated on a ministry assignment, getting married to someone outside the local fold, or died.

At work, success looked like having a solid pension plan, medical benefits, and if they were truly ambitious, an office with a door. If that wasn't attainable, being a responsible adult meant committing to a job that paid the bills until they earned that twenty-five-year pin, fifty-year commemorative watch, or fifty-pound retirement turkey (I don't know; I just remember my father bringing home a really huge turkey from work, and it seemed to be a big deal). This may still be the standard of success for some.

I am better for the loyalty I saw those around me give to their local church, jobs, and relationships. I come from the generation that proudly stayed. Sadly, many of them did so through abusive marriages, spiritually toxic leadership, and unfulfilling jobs. Commitment was pitted against choice without them realizing that "sticking with it" was also a choice worth evaluating.

You have some evaluating to do too. You get to decide which principles are worth repeating in your life and which ones are worth rejecting. The weight of that decision is made so much lighter as you commit to being transformed by God's Word and trusting when Holy Spirit is leading you in a new direction.

Perhaps you've always stayed home with the kids and now you feel you could best serve your family outside the home. Alternatively you might be like women I know who have chosen the opposite. I've coached women with thriving careers outside the home. Women who were six- and seven-figure earners who started to feel a calling to serve their family by staying at home. How courageous! Then there is Yvonne Orji. In her final year of medical school, Yvonne changed gears to pursue—wait for it—comedy. In her book, *Bamboozled by Jesus*, she shares how she felt God leading her down this new and never-explored path. Orji has since been nominated for a Primetime Emmy Award and multiple NAACP Image Awards.

I would like you to hone in on the messages you received about the fundamental freedom to change your mind! You are not inconsistent. I revoke that diagnosis. You may need to place this book down momentarily, square your shoulders, and shout it out loud: "I am not inconsistent!" You need to audibly hear that after years of being misunderstood and ill-spoken of. You must always be insistent about obeying that seemingly nonsensical tugging of Holy Spirit on your heart, even when it bids you to chart a completely new course.

I have been stewarding a prophetic word I received over ten years ago about the fluidity of a purpose-led life. I feel released to responsibly pass it on to you. Here it is: "The decision you are faced with is not *Is God calling me?* Rather, your decision is a matter of where. You will be placed strategically in God's army as He has need for you, and you must learn how to discern when it is time to move." This can look like pulling up roots you have put down or a career change. It can also be less intrusive and sound like *I have changed my mind.*

You must become critically aware of how you were socialized to view choice and commitment. This could be the key to understanding why you stay, stray, or get stuck when dealing with big-*C* change.

I believe in commitment. It is biblical, and our society could use an influx of it. But as I've studied the Word of God, I've also observed a recurring life cycle of seasons, change, and God doing a new thing (see Ecclesiastes 3:1; Isaiah 43:19). When you have limited examples or celebrations of nontraditional paths to purpose-led living (such as entrepreneurship, the arts, or being a wife, mother, and itinerant speaker), your thoughts about purpose and service, if not unboxed, are left to be curated by the unchallenged and false reality that God presents you with only one right option in this life, so you better choose accurately because that choice is final.

What a limited perspective. Perhaps you are held up by some of the same binding belief systems too. The fear of choosing wrong has led many to late starts, indecision, or inaction. Living by the idea that you cannot call for a plot change in the middle of your own life story and making peace with staying out of fear of the audience walking out on you is like taking small doses of cyanide every day until you meet your untimely end while insisting that you are taking vitamins. This perspective is not enhancing your life; it is eroding it.

But guess what?

You can shift it.

I know those four words are freeing you right now. You've been reading this not realizing your deep need for permission to make a move. That stirring you have been experiencing is not rebellion; it is your release!

4. You Can Never Say No When Asked to Do Something for God

This message is wrong for a few reasons:

- *God* and *church* should never be used interchangeably.
- Someone else cannot decide for you what God wants you to do.
- This type of messaging fosters a sense of legality instead of liberality. God wants us to give from a willing heart. Paul writes about this in his letter to the believers in Corinth:

> The point is this: whoever sows sparingly will also reap sparingly, and whoever sows bountifully will also reap bountifully. Each one must give as he has decided in his heart, not reluctantly or under compulsion, for God loves a cheerful giver.
> 2 CORINTHIANS 9:6-7

I don't know about you, but I want in on that bounty!

This binding belief also conditions the hearer to believe that a yes to humans is always the same thing as a yes to God. It dulls your personal hunger and ability to hear from God for yourself. Yes, you. You can hear God for yourself! God wants to speak, can speak, and is speaking directly to *you*.

Acts 2:17 speaks to this clearly through these words from the prophet Joel: "In the last days it shall be, God declares, that I will pour out my Spirit on all flesh, and your sons and your daughters shall prophesy, and your young men shall see visions, and your old men shall dream dreams."

This is not an obedience debate. Hands down, we are called to serve. That point is not being challenged. But the belief system communicated to me—whenever you are asked to do something for God, you should never say no—made me feel pressured. That pressure became feelings of guilt. Those feelings became the message that God doesn't care about the individual; He wants mindless devotion. And that message became an emotional stronghold that sucked the joy out of serving and turned it into a loveless act of conformity.

We hear with our heart and filter through our experiences. I want to invite you to open your heart to receive a new message about living a purpose-filled life: *Whatever God is asking you to do, there is joy and peace in your yes.*

Need more convincing?

> All the promises of God find their Yes in him. That is why it is through him that we utter our Amen to God for his glory.
>
> 2 CORINTHIANS 1:20

> You make known to me the path of life;
> in your presence there is fullness of joy;
> at your right hand are pleasures forevermore.
>
> PSALM 16:11

> The kingdom of God is not a matter of eating and drinking but of righteousness and peace and joy in the Holy Spirit.
>
> ROMANS 14:17

Let these truths excite you. Let these words cause you to feel joy. Let this feeling of joy become a new message: *There is contentment in serving God.* And lastly, let this message become a spiritual discipline that governs how you utilize your gifts, resources, and time.

5. People Are Depending on You

The super-shero pep talk "They're all depending on you" is often used to motivate; however, if ever the ego had a time of feasting, it is on these words. I have watched churches, companies, relationships, and individuals hit burnout, grow resentful, or collapse because of this super-shero approach to life. I have personally lived under its weight. It meant I could not fail. And guess what? I was going to fail, I did fail, and you will fail too. I know it's been asked before, but can we normalize failure? Not sin but failure. Somewhere along the way we've made the two interchangeable.

I remember the first time I received an invitation to speak at a church. "People are depending on you" echoed in my ears. I pictured households of people fasting and faith rising because the congregation needed something from God (true), and I was going to be the one responsible for delivering it (false). One of my professors shared these words with me, and they have never left my consciousness: "You are a pit stop on their journey, and you are not responsible for the whole. Just do your part."

Those people were depending on God, not on me. We are not the only ones who need this reminder from time to time. The apostle Paul provided his pupils with a similar pep talk when he said, "I planted, Apollos watered, but God gave the growth. So neither he who plants nor he who waters is anything, but only God who gives the growth. He who plants and he who waters are one, and each will receive his wages according to his labor" (1 Corinthians 3:6-8).

You are tasked with being obedient in using your gifts and entrusting the rest to God. What a liberating reminder! It's not on you; He just wants what's in you. Use what's in your hand, staying in your lane. Shift your mindset, be kind to yourself, and bind belief systems that aren't serving you well.

6. If It Doesn't Work Out, It Wasn't Meant to Be

You can obey God and still meet resistance, calamity, and hardship. It's not said nearly enough, but it's true. Since childhood, I have constantly heard people around me accepting resistance as an indication that what they were pursuing was probably not what God wanted for them. That way of thinking taught me not to push. It encouraged me to change lanes every time the ride got bumpy. That *Oh well, this must not be for me* mentality robbed me of so many opportunities because the message being sent was that if it was God's will for me, it would just come to me. Ease was considered the stamp of God's approval. But this is not so. Dis-ease is not rejection. Dis-ease is oftentimes life just doing what it is going to do—push back, act up, and be unpredictable. Dis-ease is commonly the infliction that causes the complacent and the cowardly to activate their POUR (**p**otential **o**therwise **u**nder**r**ealized).

God is more concerned with your character than He is with your comfort. This means He will allow you to break a sweat in order to break a curse, bad habit, or unproductive pattern to mature your faith and purpose. He is not trying to make you beg for it; He is trying to make you better for it because you were already built for it.

You will have to knock on doors more than once while obeying your call. God can tell you to go back to school and then you might not be accepted into one of the first programs you apply for. Let's stop spiritualizing resistance as God not wanting us to do something. Breaking, crushing, and pushing are themes we see throughout Scripture (Psalm 34:17-19; Romans 5:3-5; James 1:2-4).

I've made peace with the fact that failing—at some point and at some things—is inevitable. No is to be expected, and pressing is for our good. May God grant you the grace to be a finisher. May He break every historical and generational pattern of stopping prematurely, in Jesus' name!

Do not read on in a haste after such a prophetic declaration. Take a few moments to allow it to seep into your soul like cool rain over freshly tilled soil. All the inner tousling you experienced before picking up this book has been aerating the surface of your heart so the rain can trickle right on in.

The thought that we won't experience resistance is how comfort zones are formed, and comfort zones are a nesting place for fears and insecurities. I count it a privilege to be used to expose the lie and equip you to live your wildest dreams.

We could have spent the first half of this chapter covering six lessons I have learned about life and love and why I am better for them. We will get to the motivational stuff momentarily. But we must determine the shape we are in before we continue to pour anything else in. By the time you are turning the last page of this book, I want you to be able to place it down feeling full, clear, and resolved. Therefore, we must unbox one aspect of our curated self at a time.

Growing Pains

You, my friend, have grown up and grown out of the box you are in. At this intersection of your life, "Because I said so" will not cut it anymore. As you get ready to pack up and move on from this place, you need to decide what goes in the moving pile and what you will put out on the curb. Second Corinthians 10:5 gives us a nice head start on that list of things that need to go: "We destroy arguments and every lofty opinion raised against the knowledge of God, and take every thought captive to obey Christ."

It is time to take inventory of the binding and unbiblical belief systems that have served your curated self but stifled your created self all these years. I invite you to take out a pen and, in your journal that you have designated for unboxing, write down one binding belief system that is keeping you stuck and stagnant. Now write down three truths to your lie. It's okay if you need to ask for help to identify what truth looks like if you are not in the habit of regular introspection. Apply and repeat.

My journal entry looks something like this:

Old Message: If I receive help, it will be thrown back in my face.

New Message: Receiving help does not make me weak; it makes me stronger.

New Message: Someone's claim to my "fame" neither adds to nor takes away from who I am.

New Message: God assigned Kingdom partners to be a blessing to me, and I humbly receive them.

Disclaimer: This is a belief system I have to constantly guard against finding its way back into my thoughts, emotions, perspectives, and identity. You will have some sore spots that easily get triggered that you cannot afford to leave unchecked on a regular basis. They will either make you bitter or better. I dare you to take this exercise to the next level! Set a reminder in your calendar to do a heart-and-mind check twenty-one days from today.

In order to outgrow these unprofitable and petty ways of thinking (and, ultimately, living) you must start holding your theology, ideas, and thinking up to the Word of God and not rely solely on the words others have spoken, no matter how trusted the source is. That includes this book. We have built our faith and identity on the revelation others receive from God, but what you are poised for—living a purpose-filled life—requires you to divide and discern truth for yourself.

I am a church baby. Outside of a serious season of disobedience, I can't remember a time I wasn't in church. But that season of disobedience was a destiny changer. I pushed my created self to the side, which gave way to spiritual and identity dissonance. I surrounded myself with people and a lifestyle that did not align with my biblical values, and that new way of being took a toll on my being.

Have you ever been outside of yourself? Not an actual out-of-body experience, but outside yourself to the point where you were just so misaligned with your created self that you no longer recognized the person you had become? I have been there.

We often envision a backslider as one who is no longer walking in the way, but what about the one who unintentionally chose the wrong way? To that one and to everyone, I say: Your missteps are redeemable.

Here is a foundational belief system we can stand on to align us with our created self: My mistakes do not cancel my purpose. Let's look at this point in detail.

My Mistakes Do *Not* Cancel My Purpose

A lifestyle of promiscuity was what I used to pacify loneliness. It was my misguided attempt to regain power in my life. God would provide real-time ways of escape like He describes in 1 Corinthians 10:13, but I would silence anything that convicted me of doing what my wounded self desired. I would drink alone until I passed out because the life I had curated could only be experienced in short doses.

One day after a shameful plea for time and attention from my then suitor, I got a glimpse of who I had become, and I made a decision: I didn't want to be her anymore. I had a vision of myself lying on my back at the bottom of a dusty pit. I looked down at myself and asked, "How did you get here?"

After I got up from that place in my life, God's forgiveness met me with such a quickness it felt like there was never a rift. He forgave me and had already been waiting for me with open arms. He was ready to pick up where we had left off. However, I was convinced that my missteps meant that I had missed out on the better part of the life God had destined for me to live. I accepted His invitation to come back into obedient fellowship, but I also resigned myself to just being in the house (church) as a quiet little church mouse who had found her way back home. I was content to just hold my pew and my peace. But those childhood report cards had never lied. Keeping quiet was never my strong suit.

Here's the thing: "The gifts and the calling of God are irrevocable" (Romans 11:29). While I held my pew, my purpose was surfacing. Courage and confidence were rising. It was as though God prepared for my drifting by padding my purpose with extra buoyancy. I was feeling what the prophet Ezekiel must have felt: An unquenchable fire was racing within me, and its flames could not be smothered. Purpose coursed through my bones where marrow should be, and it felt like lava brimming to the point of eruption. It was still there. She was still in there! My created self still existed, and my mistakes did not cancel my purpose.

Even with all this inner incitement, I had become so comfortable with sitting down, shutting in, and shutting up. Plus, there was a peanut gallery of people whose twisted theology and faces demanded I sit, and hell was watching in hopeful anticipation that the bet it had wagered against me was about to be cashed in.

Hell lost that wager, and it has lost its bet on you, too.

I timidly started a new journey with God to get me back in alignment with my created self and back into my purpose. I slipped into and out of seasons of suppression, dumbing down my presence, and silencing my laughter, insights, and contributions. I sat in meetings bursting with ideas, staring blankly while others had conversations about problems I had solutions to, and I swallowed prophetic words that rooms full of people were praying to receive. I had been broken, and I felt like a tainted joke.

But suppression is a double-edged sword. I remember being in labor with my son. After almost twenty hours of intense contractions, it was time to push. When that baby started coming, I closed my legs and told the nurse I had changed my mind and I wanted to go home. I'll never forget her words: "If you clench your legs, you will hurt yourself and the baby." It was too late to hold back what was already in motion. Trying to hold him back was dangerous for both of us. In the midst of such a painful experience, something beautiful was making its way forth, and I was the carrier.

It is possible to be broken and a blessing at the same time.

No one is talking about getting up while you are still wounded and bleeding and insisting on leading, making a mess of others. But you can move forward from being once broken to mending and lending your gifts to the world.

Take an exhale right here and declare this aloud with me: "I am useful!"

The Bible is filled with accounts of still-useful people. One such person is an enslaved man named Onesimus. Onesimus ran away from his enslaver and ended up in Rome. There he encountered the apostle Paul and, after hearing his preaching, received Jesus Christ. His newfound relationship with Jesus changed him so much so that in the book of Philemon, we find Paul advocating for healing and reconciliation between Onesimus and his former-enslaver-now-turned-ally!

> Formerly he was useless to you, but now he has become useful both to you and to me.
>
> I am sending him—who is my very heart—back to you. I would have liked to keep him with me so that he could take your place in helping me while I am in chains for the gospel. But I did not want to do anything without your consent, so that any favor you do would not seem forced but would be voluntary. Perhaps the reason he was separated from you for a little while was

> that you might have him back forever—no longer as a slave, but better than a slave, as a dear brother.
>
> PHILEMON 1:11-16, NIV

A beautiful twist. Onesimus's very name means "useful." Onesimus's escape from enslavement was seen as a crime during his time. But even with a socially unacceptable mark on his name, it was his created identity—useful—that still prevailed. Even with our mistakes, we can still step into our place of usefulness. Jesus, our advocate, is pleading to the Father on our behalf (Romans 8:34; 1 John 2:1). We can return to our place of service, and we are still useful to the King. The Word of God changes us and is changing us. We are constantly being prepared, polished, and propelled.

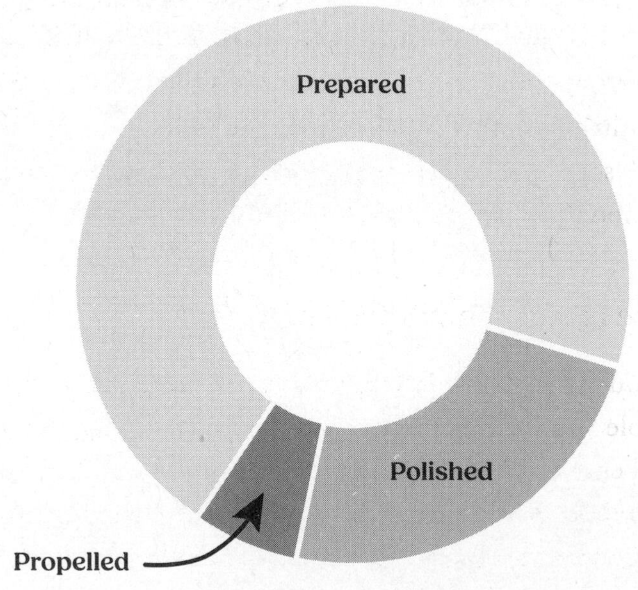

I thought the goal was to be perfect. I didn't understand then that sanctification and holiness are a process and a continual work of being perfected. I didn't understand that not only can we come into relationship with Jesus carrying all our broken pieces, but after being made whole, we will find ourselves broken again and again while still in His hands (Jeremiah 18:1-4). No one showed me their scars, proof that life had broken them or that maybe their own disobedience, ignorance, or arrogance had led them into ditches that fractured their faith and identity. Oh, how I longed to see some scars—a few battle wounds that would let me know someone else carried contradictions, lived through imperfections, yet God was able to repurpose what seemed disposable and still craft their life into something worth using. I had to learn the hard way the delicate two-step that holiness and grace seemed to share. Two steps forward, walk upright. Two steps left, no one is perfect. Two steps to the right, you are doing better than it seems. Swaying to the rhythm of God's heartbeat, a song of acceptance whose lyrics have been written with blood.

Dance Like Nobody's Watching

Do you have two left feet? Stumble, my faithful sister. Stumble your way to your created self. You have not come to the end of yourself. You have come to the end of your *curated* self. Every great invention or scientific breakthrough went through a series of iterations before reaching its performance peak. Even then, there are countless recalls or user updates.

God is working out your kinks, and He would not put in that kind of time and energy just to put you in the trash because of a performance error. This kind of investment screams, "I know she has the potential to be more!"

It may not seem like it right now, but you are being prepared, polished, and propelled into your calling. I release this declaration over you from 1 Peter 5:10: "After you have suffered a little while [*prepared*], the God of all grace, who has called you to his eternal glory in Christ, will himself restore, confirm, strengthen [*polished*], and establish [*propelled*] you."

Chapter Check-In

What have you heard that is now speaking for you? Conversations and indirect messages that have resurfaced and interject *No*, *Can't*, *Won't*, or *Not possible* before you can even process what is happening and make a sound decision for yourself. I want to encourage you to challenge those messages and prayerfully allow Holy Spirit to guide you in doing the work outlined in this chapter to let them go. You can do it. I have confidence in you.

Journal Prompt: I know this belief is not true, but it makes me comfortable to continue believing . . .

Remember: You must always be insistent about obeying that seemingly nonsensical tugging of Holy Spirit on your heart, even when it bids you to chart a completely new course.

3
The Box You've Outgrown
Unboxing Your Relationships

To be in any sort of relationship where you do not express yourself, simply to keep the peace, is a relationship ruled by one person and will never be balanced or healthy.

BRONNIE WARE

I don't mean to be superficial, but one of my most devastating experiences was outgrowing my favorite pair of light-blue jeans. I could dress them up or turn them into the perfect comfy, casual look. I loved them because they were a no-brainer staple item to go to, and the fit was incredible. Those jeans covered what didn't need to be shared, minimized what the world didn't need to know I had in abundance, and accentuated just enough curves to be sexy and tasteful at the same time. I loved how I looked in those jeans. They made me feel confident, comfortable, and ready for anything. I didn't care if the dress code called for formal attire, if those jeans were clean and I was in the mood for them, I was wearing them to fit the occasion. Bloated or snatched, I felt like my best self in those light-blue jeans.

But one day those jeans with the perfect amount of stretch just didn't fit. No amount of sucking in or jumping up and down was going to get me into those jeans. I gathered reinforcement and put on my best shapewear, which flattened me in all the right places, and yet there was still no room to fit into that perfect pair of light-blue jeans. You have to understand: I am thick, fluffy, and petite. The perfect-fitting pair of anything is an anomaly. I don't just buy a new pair of jeans, I tarry for one until it appears (I know, super melodramatic, but if you know, you know). And because the struggle is so very real, in this moment I feel not one ounce of shame giving this complete and full disclosure—I even considered wearing them with only the top button fastened, the zipper wide open, a long flowy shirt, and the inevitable pending shame of being exposed, just to get the final honorary strut in that light-blue pair of jeans.

Can you picture what a hot mess I would have looked like walking around in a pair of tight jeans barely shimmied over my buttocks, front wide open, and a blousy shirt as my only line of defense? What a picture of catastrophe and discomfort.

I would have been the brunt of a random people watcher's joke. I know this because I enjoy observing the fashion choices of busy passersby. When I see a look that seems oddly out of my norm, I think to myself, *I'd love to know the story behind that outfit choice. What was their inner conversation when they purchased that outfit or pulled that look together?* The dialogue I was having with myself as I truly contemplated that embarrassing blue jeans mash-up was *I don't want to let go because putting in the work and money for a new pair seems daunting and unlikely to result in success.* Success or failure aside, I had to come to terms with letting those jeans go.

Walking in your purpose will require moving on from some people and places that in this season have you looking like that picture of catastrophe and discomfort. You must come to terms with the expense, time, and loss of obeying God and let them go. They haven't fit for a while. No amount of dumbing down your created self or compromising to be accepted is going to do the trick. Conformity has done its best to keep your created attributes from being a disruption to some, and you still have not found success rekindling the groove you once experienced and appreciated in those places. You loved them because they were a no-brainer go-to, and you loved how being with them made you look and feel. But one day you realized they just don't fit.

If only "they" were a pair of jeans, you would have gladly retired them and purchased a new pair a long time ago. But instead of an article of clothing, we are talking about people, relationships, history, community, and seemingly your identity, too. We are also talking about possibly leaving your job or church, moving to another province or state, closing the doors on your business, or letting a friendship go. These connections seem to have grown an umbilical cord, and severing them feels like losing your lifeline. Aligning this part of your life with your created self might be the hardest adjustment you will have to make. You've known it for some time. You wanted them to be the one to launch you, see you, understand you, affirm you, or mentor you. Your fondest memories include these places and people, and moving on from them feels sinister. They served a season of your life well. You may not have caught a glimpse of your created self without them, but you most certainly cannot tap into where God is taking you without the courage and the obedience to move on.

Here are some myth busters about moving on that you need to know if you are going to find the courage to move on in obedience and not shelter what needs to be severed:

- Moving on is not an indictment of the people and places you are leaving. It is an indication that you are healing and hearing from God concerning your next steps.
- The feeling of *I've outgrown this relationship* is not an insult. It can be articulated as "I need something else" over "I need something better," or "I need you and . . ." instead of "I need more."

- You are not responsible for helping someone else sort through how they feel about you ending the relationship. Let go of that sense of responsibility to soothe those you move on from.

I can hear someone's wheels turning and them asking, "Well, can't I reconnect with them from time to time?" The answer: "No. Not right now." And the truth is, maybe not ever. I feel the need to speak in absolutes because I am speaking directly to the woman who already struggles with moving on and holding on, and it is costing you time and compromising your very soul. Here's a confession: There is a place I had to move on from, and I would often visit out of guilt. Every time I was there, I felt this sinking feeling in the pit of my stomach, and I felt horrible about myself upon leaving. My created self took a hit. I'm sure my visit was giving someone else life, but for me, it felt like the onset of death. This went on for at least four years. On my last visit to the burial site (that's what it felt like), I told myself quietly, *Yep, this is going to be my last visit*. Even as I am typing this, I hear Holy Spirit asking, "Why do you seek the living among the dead?" (Luke 24:5). Moving on means having the courage to go—and the courage not to go back.

When God starts stirring you to move on from the people and places you call home, it can be too painful to confront. It's one thing to acknowledge how the actions of others have contributed to shaping your curated self. With Jesus and therapy, you can identify how the words of a former boss or your fourth-grade teacher are the reason why you doubted your greatness all those years. That mental block was not your fault. That is on them, not you. But it requires a deeper personal level of vulnerability, honesty, and ownership to acknowledge that your current fruitfulness is being delayed by your own hands. Attempting to coddle your insecurities about stepping into alignment with your created self, you have pacified your budding purpose by remaining in comfort zones God has told you to leave and by drowning out the conviction of Holy Spirit with the noise of the crowd.

This chapter was by far the most difficult for me to write. I had areas of my own life that still needed to come into obedience with the chapter's contents before I was released to continue writing it.

Every time I sat down to write, I felt stuck and confused. I realized I was undergoing my own unboxing experience. There were some people and places that I held close to my heart and proudly attributed my success and value to. I could drop a name or reference an affiliation and go from feeling overlooked to being treated like the most important person in the room. So when God said it was time to move, I prioritized my comfort over obeying God as He called me in another direction. I was paralyzed as I obsessed over thoughts like *What would I tell them? What will people think? Will I lose relationships? Who will I be without being in proximity to them?* To add insult to injury, God was asking me to move when He hadn't even told me what He was up to or where I was going next!

Is God nudging you into the unknown? Has the paralysis of analysis produced inaction in your life? Are you rehearsing all the possible *What if . . . ?* scenarios moving on might produce? Walking in your purpose will mean making faith moves with no forwarding address. It may even feel like you've been benched or downsized. Sometimes moving on doesn't feel like moving on at all. Sometimes moving on feels like losing.

One day while trying to string together clear thoughts for this chapter, I popped straight up from my desk like someone was doing a roll call and I needed to yell "Present!" No exaggeration. I realized the reason for my writer's block. God could not use me to lead others into victory over an area I had not completely subdued. It wasn't top of mind, nor was I being willfully disobedient. It was more like conveniently ignoring, no, deferring—I like deferring better—my obedience to moving on. Either way, I had not confronted the stack of eviction notices God had been posting on the entrance of my own comfort zone. Without any further delay, I set into motion every resignation, cancellation, and "I regret to inform you" conversation I needed to have before the close of the day.

Can you guess what happened next? The floodgates opened! This chapter went from being the most difficult to write to revelation flowing onto the page with clarity and ease. The fruitfulness of this work was being delayed by my own hands.

What about your hands? Are they helping build you

or bind you? It's natural to want to protect and preserve the things that are important to us. But with God, please know He promises this: "Whoever would save his life will lose it, but whoever loses his life for my sake will find it" (Matthew 16:25).

I would never share something with you I haven't tried, tested, and proven for myself. I lost a lot that day. I'm still working through the grief associated with losing what I loved. Obedience is not transactional. You don't give God your yes and then He promptly gives you the details of what's next. Nope. Obedience is transformational. Your yes along with your process takes you through a metamorphosis: a shifting from your curated self to your created identity. Whether you are staring at God's eviction notice or packing up obediently to make your move, you can be comforted by knowing that in God's economy, losing equals winning.

I can only imagine that if it was that difficult for me to birth this chapter, it might be just as difficult for you to work through your own unboxing of your relationships. So let's pause and pray for a dose of clarity and courage before you proceed.

Father, I am thankful that if anyone knows what it feels like to have to obey a hard request, it is You. Help us activate the holy boldness required to step out of what is familiar and move in radical faith as You align us with a greater measure of our purpose. In Jesus' name, amen.

The Cost of Not Moving

For some, the call to move comes as a feeling. A nauseating inward gnawing that won't settle with Pepto Bismol or Pepcid AC (you can tell I've tried). For others it's an audible instruction that you've been rationalizing as being your own thoughts, so you choose logic over the leading of Holy Spirit. And still there are others who are pressed through visions and dreams. Restless nights and hijacked days filled with imagery, symbols, and messages of "It's time to go!"

Yet for some unexplainable reason, we have overstayed our welcome or, worse, have tried to come up with ways to serve both visions. Where there are two visions, we have division and the collision of our created and curated selves, which only leads to the next stage: die-vision.

Ever been so misplaced that you find yourself saying, "I feel like I'm dying"? That's the onset of die-vision. In Matthew 6:24 Jesus is teaching about money but shares a transferable truth about the impact of playing two sides: "No one can serve two masters, for either he will hate the one and love the other, or he will be devoted to the one and despise the other. You cannot serve God and money."

This is why you've developed a slight disdain for what you once loved. What excited you is now draining you, and what you once felt called to now feels like an unsettling compromise. You cannot serve two masters at the same time. As you negotiate aspects of your created self, you find yourself becoming insecure, unsure about every little decision, and doubtful of the woman you were created to be. Not every move will cause you this kind of conflict. But a God-issued move that you delay responding to will certainly split you in two. It creates an internal love-hate relationship, which becomes an external love-hate relationship and, eventually, a vertical love-hate relationship.

We each have a responsibility to hold our community, accountability partners, spiritual coverings, and those we respect—whether a boss, friend, pastor, parent, or mentor—in their rightful place and not make them gods. Doing so will help us preserve our created self and curb our curated tendencies to put our confidence in the wrong places. When we elevate anyone as equal to God, consulting them before (or instead of) God, we can find ourselves putting more weight on their approval over our obedience to God. This is a sure threat to walking in our created self and maintaining purpose clarity.

Let's be clear. Submission to others is godly and God pleasing when done with a biblical perspective. But we must become wiser about what or whom we commit to because God will require us to submit to Him, too! If you truly want God to win so you can experience singularity of heart and a purpose-filled life, then unboxing your relationships will give you the ease to please the Father and surrender a timely yes when it is time for your next move.

A Culture of Transactions and Indebtedness

My mother was unrelenting about drilling gratitude into her children. Each Christmas, or on any occasion really, she would give me the same stern reminder:

"Don't forget to write a card for Sister So-and-so; she picked you up every Wednesday for Bible study."

"Don't forget to buy a gift for Brother Who-and-who; he always gives you a ride home from choir practice."

Those prompts were followed up with intermittent admonishments of "Nicole, never take it for granted when people show you kindness. They do not have to think of you."

The Bible calls for us to be grateful. "Give honor where honor is due" (Proverbs 3:27, author's paraphrase). "Pay everyone what you owe them" (Romans 13:7, CEB). There are over one hundred Bible verses on showing admiration and giving recognition where it is expected.

The book of Hebrews features an entire list of honorary faith walkers we are admonished to venerate (Hebrews 11:4-40), men and women of God who broke glass ceilings, endured unimaginable hardships, and pioneered the path before us. We must not forget them as we hold their testimonies in the highest esteem and use their lives as rich lessons and inspiration. You probably have a list of giants in your own life: a dedicated mother, a praying spiritual leader, an immigration sponsor, a business investor, a generous employer, a keep-your-secrets auntie, an all-around good shepherd whose shoulders you stand on.

This virtue and legacy of gratitude is why I am always

saddened when I read the story of the ten lepers Jesus healed (Luke 17:11-19, NIV). After being sick and socially isolated from their loved ones, all ten of the gravely ill men were healed by Jesus, who restored not only their physical health but also their social and economic well-being. Get this: Only one of the men, a Samaritan, returned to say thank-you. They all owed Him! Honor was rightfully due! Jesus went on to ask a series of rhetorical questions:

"Were not all ten cleansed?"

"Where are the other nine?"

"Has no one returned to give praise to God except this foreigner?"

The painstaking audacity of it all (my words, not His)! Jesus knew good and well that the others had been healed. He lays in on them this way not to highlight the ingratitude of the nine but to cause the Samaritan to recognize that his gratitude was not being taken lightly. What he was doing was honorable. The former leper was showing honor where it was due.

With as much as these men had received, all Jesus required was their acknowledgment and thankfulness to God. He didn't ask them to follow Him because of it, nor did He make them bond servants (people who are bound to service with no compensation). In fact, at the end of His conversation with the Samaritan, Jesus says, "Rise and go." That's it! This moment speaks more profoundly than we may perceive at first glance. We see no debt being placed on the man. If there was ever a dynamic where one person should owe the other, it was this one. Jesus receives the Samaritan's thanksgiving as the appropriate response to kindness, showing that even when there is a power imbalance in an interaction, saying thank-you is enough.

Jesus' conversation with the healed man leaves me asking some questions about gratitude. A traced handprint on construction paper with the misspelled sentiment "Tank U" written in crayon is cute and acceptable from a five-year-old, but there are vastly different expectations for how adults should express gratitude. Why has gratitude become a noose around the necks of so many? Why do so many of us show and sow kindness only to later place a tab on it that was not in the fine print or previously communicated to the beneficiary? Droves of misplaced and misaligned people have confused guilt for gratitude and are now bound to people who at the appointed time, should have followed Jesus' lead and released them.

Kindness is a seed to be planted, not a debt to be repaid. I pray that this is freeing for you to read, whether you feel forever indebted to someone or have a few people you need to release from your heart's secret "you owe me" jail.

The idea of being emotionally indebted (not financially; pay what you owe) to anyone has no biblical legs to stand on. Love gives (John 3:16). You are not required to match the level of kindness you are shown or repay it beyond a heartfelt thank-you. If any payment is required, it is to pay it forward, and if someone expects something different, that is not love; it is leverage. Roxanne Francis, lead therapist and CEO of Francis Psychotherapy, explained to me that "Healthy relationships are unconditional. Whether or not you have something to give, that person should still be there."[1]

For clarity, allow me to state the maybe-not-so-obvious. There is nothing wrong with wanting to show a thoughtful gesture when someone is a blessing in our lives; after all, it is biblical to give honor where honor is due. However, beware of wanting to repay kindness with more kindness because of deep-seated insecurity or wounded pride that prevents you from knowing how to stand still and be blessed.

Guilt or Gratitude

Here are five red flags that your gratitude may, in fact, be driven by guilt:

HOW TO DETECT IF YOU ARE MOTIVATED BY *guilt* OR GRATITUDE

Guilt Says	Gratitude Says
"I owe you."	"I appreciate you."
"I have to . . ."	"I am happy to . . ."
"They will be mad."	"They will understand."
"I should . . ."	"I get to . . ."
"I don't deserve this."	"Thank you."

There is a grace allotted for the people and places you are assigned to in the season you are assigned to them. Guilt will keep you tied to people and places long after grace has moved on. Purpose requires you to know when that grace has lifted before your called-to place becomes a place of confinement. Where grace goes your created self flows. There is an oil (divine enablement) for your assignment. It will increase your reach, level of impact, and effectiveness. When the prophet Samuel went to anoint the next king, no matter who stood before him, God told him not to pour the oil until the right person showed up (1 Samuel 16).

Are you showing up as the right person, or is your curated counterfeit still trying to usurp your created self? Have you outserved your present job, title, or circle?

Take a moment to make your own guilt-free gratitude list. Prayerfully consider some of the people and places that have been a blessing to you. Who has shown you favor or showered you with kindness? Who called your name in rooms you would have never been invited into or made you feel seen and affirmed? Now write them down in the space on the next page and ask Holy Spirit to reveal to you (1) whom to honor; (2) how to honor them; and (3) whom to let go. Letting go may involve a clean break or a bit of distance and space. Let Holy Spirit be the One to inform you which one needs to take place in order to make the move into your new grace.

My Gratitude List

God is doing a new thing in you, and He has made it crystal clear that you can't take everyone with you. Even though your heart will forever be filled with gratitude, the kindness you were shown can no longer be used as a comma where there should be a period.

Period.

Celebration and Validation Culture

Being validated and celebrated feels so good. Whether it comes in the form of likes on a social-media page, a stellar performance review at work, or that passerby who yells, "I love your hair," we can feel our self-esteem rising by degrees. Science proves validation and celebration are beneficial,[2] and psychology says we need it to reach our highest version of self-actualization. Proverbs 12:25 tells us that a good word makes one's heart glad, and Proverbs 15:23 boasts, "A man has joy in an apt answer, And how delightful is a timely word!" (NASB 1995).

Why then would anyone willingly give up the safety of the people and places that know us best, who celebrate how amazing we are and provide us with a sense of meaning and identity? The answer: increase. Increase in your current perception of God, yourself, and your situation. Abraham got that glimpse of more on that starry night on the beach with God (Genesis 15), and when you get that kind of revelation, it becomes increasingly difficult to stay put.

In Genesis 12:1-9, we read where God granted Abraham a vision of his future. God showed him a blessing so large he couldn't even quantify it. But to step into it, Abraham had to pursue a promise that was waiting for him in a place he had never been and with a people he shared no intimate history with. He didn't even know where it was! Abraham had roots where he was. He knew the lay of the land, literally. In obedience, not having any clue where he was going, he set out in the complexity of a vision and word from God about his destiny. He had no road map to get there other than the instruction to go, but he trusted the One who told him it was time to move.

Can you relate to Abraham? God has shown you that there is more than "this." You may not have seen it in a vision. Maybe you felt it in your gut. But there is no arguing that God has spoken, and what's lying ahead is going to be BIG.

We all want it: to move from this to that, from good to great, from ordinary to extraordinary. We're not in a competitive climb to the top; we're just moving to the best version of ourselves, our created selves. We want to interrupt generational patterns, create generational wealth, and make His name glorious.

You've glimpsed it and even gotten a taste of it. Yet you are still here in this place called familiar and with these people you know all too well, struggling with the big "C" called codependency.

Codependency is defined by the *Merriam-Webster* dictionary as "a relationship in which a person manifesting low self-esteem and a strong desire for approval has an unhealthy attachment to another."[3] You've convinced yourself that *they* need you. Leaving now is not a good time for *them*. But maybe it's your curated self that really needs *them*.

God confronted me with a really difficult question. He said, *What if after all the late nights, struggling, sacrifices, and investments to help women step into their created self, you never get public praise for it but it paves the way for someone else. Would you still do it?* It knocked the wind out of me. I'll share this ultraintrospective question with you, too. With all the lifelong work that goes into living a life of purpose, if no one stops to acknowledge your impact or efforts, would you still commit to it? God wants your no-strings-attached yes! But giving it daily can be difficult because of our addiction to outward success and praise.

We can grow addicted to being liked, even loved, and

being on top. And we fear walking into a new season where we may not be seen, celebrated, or known. I can hear someone saying, "I'm fine all by myself." But have you ever preached a sermon, sung a song, worked all night on a presentation, cooked a meal fit for a king only to have your best efforts go uncelebrated? That is a recipe for *Don't nobody ask me to do anything again* if I've ever seen one. In order for your created self to flourish, you will need to put your big-girl pants on and confront your insatiable appetite for celebration and validation. When the cheers grow silent around you, know that folks are not always shutting you out. Sometimes God is shutting them up to kill your appetite before it kills you.

As God is unboxing you, there are some things He wants to download to you about your next assignment that you will not hear until you come away from the clamor of "Well done" and the affirmation of "There's such an anointing on your life." You need to know what it feels like to go without the praise because walking in purpose will demand you get up without it.

If praise is your indicator of progress, you are misinformed and may even be misaligned. Your created self thrives in the Holy Place, not the holler. It is in the Holy Place that you are filled and fueled by divine revelation from God about WHO you are. Your WHO will be able to recognize your do, what you should be using your gifts for. Some days, people will clap for you and some days you will go without the applause. Both days your purpose is still true. In this new place, we follow vision, not validation.

No one clapped when Jesus announced that He had to go to the cross. When He could have used validation, His circle fell asleep. When purpose met excruciating pain and silence, His resolve was "Not my will, but yours, be done" (Luke 22:42). Pleasing God must become enough.

Your Need to Explain

When you are convinced about your own path of obedience, you don't struggle with the need to convince others. If you have a regular need to spell things out, clarify your actions, or justify your choices (to others or yourself), you may be struggling with a fear of being rejected that comes from having been rejected in the past.

I asked my colleague Roxanne Francis for her clinical definition of *rejection*. She defined it as "the act of not being included or deliberately being removed from a circle where you would normally be included." She further shared, "It leaves the feeling of unworthiness, this feeling of *Something is wrong with me*. And what I see a lot with my clients who have experienced rejection is people-pleasing and constantly searching for validation."[4]

Rejection either demands respect or details its way into being respected and received by overexplaining its every move. The explainer uses her words like probes trying to fish out an "atta girl" because for the explainer, pleasing God has not become enough. Three of the most common types of explainers include

- **the insecure explainer**, who seeks validation;
- **the confused explainer**, who seeks affirmation;
- **the egotistical explainer**, who seeks glorification.

Excessive explaining never satisfies your deep need to be validated, affirmed, or honored and praised. It undermines the authority of God's leadership in your life and minimizes the value of your own voice. The common root here is *the need to be seen.*

The dismissal and abandonment we feel when we are rejected destabilizes us. In an attempt to stabilize our psychological need to belong, we can find ourselves grasping the wrong things and people. When we experience rejection on any level, the image of our created self is instantly cracked, leaving us with a distorted view of ourselves. Chronic explaining is just one of the coping mechanisms we develop in an attempt to substantiate our uncertainties about ourselves. We feel compelled to provide an explanation until we see a glimmer of recognition in the listener's eyes or some small gesture of affirmation that we are right, loved, and accepted—and that we belong.

This quest for recognition is known as mirroring, a process I further learned about in my conversation with therapist Roxanne. She shared: "Very early brain development is strongly dependent on this mirroring that happens when the caregiver looks at the infant. The infant needs that. The reason it's called mirroring is because when we gaze into their face, that baby looks at the adult and gets a sense of who they are from that eye-to-eye connection, and from that gaze they get the sense that *I am loved, I am safe, I am worthy, I am connected.* Humans have a sense of who we are because of that communication and connection. When there is rejection, we lose our identity. We don't know who we are. There is no place from which to be grounded. There is no center. From the breast to the bottle, there is this cradling, and you have to look at the infant. We 'coo' and we 'ah,' and the child learns to laugh because we laughed with them first."

I am in awe of the complexity of God. To consider that He would take what we now call mirroring and put that identity bond in the gaze between a parent and a newborn child. What an extraordinary depiction of the mirroring that happens when you and I, as God's very own children, gaze into His eyes and are grounded.

Consider how your worship or time spent reading the Word centers you in your emotions, thoughts, perspective, and—most importantly—your identity. The brokenness of our world has resulted in the identity bonding that mirroring provides to sometimes require an alternate caregiver due to the unavoidable (or, sometimes, intentional) absence of a parent. However, the same grounding and recognition does not happen when a nurse picks a baby up because what makes looking at the biological parent the most powerful is that they are passing on both nature and nurture. In this same way, if we look at God and consistently keep His gaze, we not only learn about His likeness but also recognize like ways in us. God is passing on both nature and nurture to us. When we find the external confirmation we sometimes seek, we are less likely to obey God and find it more and more difficult to take action (aka feel stuck). Remember, validation is not your green light, vision is.

Roxanne had more to say about the effects of rejection on our decision making:

> When we experience rejection, especially more than once, we start to believe that we are fundamentally flawed. When that's the place from which you live, you don't make the best decisions. God's Word is a mirror. We have to be willing to read the Scriptures and let them read us. When we are operating from this place of rejection, we often feel a lot of shame, and sometimes we feel guilt. People don't often know the difference between the two. A good way to think of it is guilt says, "I've done a bad thing" and shame says, "I am a bad person." You have to separate your experiences from who you are. Your experience is based on how that person treated you, but who you are is based on God's Word.

Whatever crack rejection and neglect has created in your self-image, may it be made whole in Jesus' name.

Living into Our Created Self

So how do we stabilize and mend our image of our created self?

1. **Filter the voices that are speaking into your life.** Not everyone should have the privilege of access to you at the same level. "Blessed is the man who walks not in the counsel of the wicked, nor stands in the way of sinners, nor sits in the seat of scoffers" (Psalm 1:1).
2. **Filter your speech so that your words align with your created identity.** With your words you can reroute the course of your life, even from the messiest of places (see James 3).
3. **Filter your thought life by interrupting ideologies that conflict with your created identity and replacing them with biblically sound, life-giving truths.** "Be careful how you think; your life is shaped by your thoughts" (Proverbs 4:23, GNT).

Here are five affirmations to hold on to while you are mending. Write them, recite them, and make them your own.

- I don't need others to see me in order for me to see myself.

- Among the billions of people in the world, God sees me.
- I am the one God left the ninety-nine for.
- I have a seat at the Master's table.
- God delights in me.
- There are more people for me than there are against me.

Seeking wise counsel before making a decision is wise and godly. However, when God says it is time to move, whether that move involves leaving a place or people, that conversation wasn't a conference call. It was a command.

Chapter Check-In

There is a grace allotted for the people and places you are assigned to in the season you are assigned to them. Guilt will keep you tied to people and places long after grace has moved on. Purpose requires you to know when that grace has lifted before your called-to place becomes a place of confinement. Have you already identified a few of those people and places? Bring them to the Lord, and pray for the courage and confidence to lovingly let them go.

Journal Prompt: God, I admit that I have been avoiding your nudges for me to move on from . . .

Remember: No one clapped when Jesus announced that He had to go to the cross. When He could have used validation, His circle fell asleep. When purpose met excruciating pain and silence, His resolve was "Not my will, but yours, be done" (Luke 22:42). Pleasing God must become enough.

4

The Box Your Life Has Curated

Unboxing Your Experiences

God does not speak to us from sight,
He speaks to us from revelation.
STEPHANIE IKE OKAFOR

My early years as a single mother were hectic. My life was full, and so was my schedule. Being a boy mom meant many hours of action cartoons and movies and active hours outdoors while managing a nine-to-five, long commutes, ministry, and a social life. Things were always busy and bustling. My father gave me a gift every mother dreams of: a summer off! He was going to Florida for the summer and asked if he could take his grandson. Ah, yes! I was counting down and making plans. Momma was getting her freedom, peace, rest, and whole life back.

They headed out in the early morning. I still have the picture of my son in his little cap and suitcase, earmarking the beginning of two months of freedom. For those first few days, instead of feeling like the carefree woman I envisioned, I began to slip into a dark depression. It was the first time in years my life was quiet, and I could hear my soul speak. She was sad and neglected. She had pains and aches she'd tried to communicate, but that active life I was living muffled her cries. There was grief I hadn't attended to and breakups I had never truly gotten over. There were esteem issues I had buried under motherhood and ministry, and for the first time in a long time, I had no one to take care of but myself, and I could barely face what I saw.

Those dark days snowballed into reckless and self-destructive behaviors. A couple of mine included drinking and smoking. For some it looks more like overworking and emotional eating. There was no noise, so I had to create some in order to escape the self I had curated. I turned the volume up with loud, unsacred music and unsavory company. Your noise may be an overbooked social or ministry life. Just to be clear: Not all noise is bad noise until it has idolatry as its motive. Why didn't I pray, call the saints, or tell Jesus what I was going through? Because all those interventions would have led to the inevitable—coming face-to-face with myself, which was a terrifying thought. After muffling my created self for so long, I was afraid she was no longer there.

It was time to unbox my experiences. I needed to understand the defining, difficult, and unpleasant life moments that had unraveled my created identity and my perception of God. You may have felt your own sense of self slipping away or the gradual shifting of your trust and confidence in both yourself and God. Want to know how I found my way back? I turned my face to God to find the courage to face myself. He is so much more gracious than we are. The apostle Paul wrote, "But he said to me, 'My grace is sufficient for you, for my power is made perfect in weakness.' Therefore I will boast all the more gladly of my weaknesses, so that the power of Christ may rest upon [or dwell in] me" (2 Corinthians 12:9).

You need God's grace to muster up the courage to unpack your divorce, betrayal, abuse, breakup, sickness, child's death, unwanted pregnancy, financial hardship, flunking out of school, being let down by a parent, failing to live up to your own or others' expectations, or simply, life plans that didn't go your way.

This does not only apply to past experiences. With every new impactful moment, you will need to pause and reposition yourself so that your created identity remains clear and not crushed . . . because clarity gives you the ability to choose wisely.

Where You Are Is Not Who You Are

When I was in labor, there was no asking, "How far apart are they?" My contractions were coming on top of each other!

I remember the nurse having such pity in her eyes as she looked at me and then the monitor. My contractions were intense and evoked pity because on the screen they looked like a cascade of waterfalls overlapping each other. As one was on the decline, another one was rising. Has your life ever felt like that? Like you just can't catch a break? After vital blows to our character, esteem, and thought life, it gets harder and harder to stand tall in who we are.

In the synoptic Gospels, we read about a woman with a chronic bleeding condition (Matthew 9:20-22; Mark 5:25-34; Luke 8:43-48). We don't know her name or where she is from. The only distinguishing detail is her condition, which she had suffered from for twelve years. She had no medical coverage. All her money had been depleted by the cost of medications and remedies. She had become an outcast, pushed to the margins of society. I can only imagine that her faith meter was running close to empty too. A woman in her situation was considered ceremonially unclean, which barred her from any interactions with the priests at times of corporate worship. It was so bad and had gone on for so long that she became known as "the woman with the issue of blood."

You will have to guard against identifying yourself by the issues you are facing or have lived through. Where you are is not who you are. Poverty, abandonment, rejection, loss, abuse, betrayal, demotion, illness, all of it. The divorce, bankruptcy, failing the exam twice, every bit of it. The Word of God boldly declares, "Do not be afraid; you will not be put to shame. Do not fear disgrace; you will not be humiliated. You will forget the shame of your youth and remember no more the reproach of your widowhood" (Isaiah 54:4, NIV). There will be days you will look around and not see any social proof that your created self ever existed. This is why you weatherproof your purpose whenever there are clear skies by writing down clarity while you have clarity. While you read this book or while riding the bus, whenever you have those God moments, when who you are is clear and that clarity makes you feel like you can conquer the world, write it down. Even if you don't think it is possible but you know God is speaking, write it down.

Here's why. When our emotions are in flux, they hijack our intellect. Everything we know to be true becomes harder to access so we go with the tide instead of the truth. When we write down moments of clarity, we are creating a wheelhouse of evidence that we can read to regain our purpose posture.

Understanding Your Storms

When you are in school, there are many prerequisites to graduating. However, none of them include how to hold on to your identity in the midst of the inevitable storms you will face.

During the first few years of our marriage, my husband and I waded through some rough financial waters. I couldn't understand. I had completed my struggle lap before we got married and demonstrated that I knew how to trust God and make faith moves whether there was a little or a lot. "I learned the lesson," I would tell God. Why was I here again in this new season of my life?

One day after one of my frustrated, honest rants with God, He answered back, "This storm is for him." God revealed that where He was going to take our lives next required my husband's pragmatism and natural nature to provide and protect to match my radical "let's drive twenty-one hours to another country with no money in our bank account because God said so" kind of faith.

When you are going through a storm, imagine that experience as a platform or stage. We find these raised platforms typically in theaters on which actors perform or speakers speak. Your storm is the platform God will use to perform a miracle in your life and elevate your perspective of Him and yourself. Losing my mother to cancer, becoming pregnant at nineteen, receiving a challenging health diagnosis, and having to move my family in the middle of winter with no first and last month's rent saved are all storms I didn't see coming or ending in my favor. But each storm has had something in common: They've all taught me new things about myself and about God. I've learned God is dependable, I'm tougher than I think, miracles do still happen, God knows what is best for me, there is a calling on my life, and the list goes on. So what storms have you had to navigate?

bankruptcy
childhood trauma
chronic mental illness
divorce
homelessness
sickness
other: ______________

God allowed the storms so that they could elevate you. Without them, you and your experience in Him would remain shallow and small.

Storms and Stages Exercise

It is easy to miss the lessons life's storms are teaching us. Take a few moments now to list a storm you have weathered or are currently weathering and the lesson you may have missed. You may have to dig deep because the more volatile the storm, the more difficult it can be to believe that it has any value. Here is a prompt to get you started.

What biblical truth has your particular storm taught you about the sovereignty of God? Alternatively, reflect on what strengths and weaknesses your storm has revealed about your character.

When we allow the storm that is going on around us to get inside us, it will sink what we were working on before the storm hit—whether it was a project or ourselves. A major part of my work as a coach is helping women identify and understand what is at the root of their patterns of starting toward a goal and then stopping. We isolate the thinking at the root of the behavior or experience and replace the binding belief system with truth from the evidence in the woman's life and God's Word.

Case Study

There we were. The end of a fabulous strategy session. My client, Angelica, had a long-held goal to create a blog for Christian bonus moms on navigating blended familyhood. Her blog was the vehicle through which she felt called to share her voice and experiences, but she just couldn't get it off the ground. Together we created a solid execution plan with links to all the resources she hadn't known how to find, complete with clear milestones and all.

Lit up with excitement and already knowing what the obvious response would be, I turned to Angelica and asked, "Soooo, how do you feel?"

"Terrible!" she replied.

You could have heard my jaw hit my keyboard. Terrible? Terrible?! It didn't make any sense. After a bit of probing, the most shocking revelation surfaced.

Setting deadlines made Angelica feel depressed and

worthless. She had tried to start her blog before, but each time a storm came or she even caught sight of a storm cloud forming, she lost momentum and eventually placed her calling on the back burner. Her storms included sickness, family conflict, marital conflict, and a barrage of criticism from the peanut gallery, who felt like her time could be better spent otherwise. With each storm, deadlines were missed, and Angelica was sucked into a whirlwind of self-loathing that was triggered each time she even thought about setting a blog-related deadline. Her binding belief system was *I am worthless, and I never complete what I start. A deadline is only a reminder of this and a setup to fail again.* This was the aftermath of a series of storms for Angelica. We began the repairs by strengthening Angelica's mental defenses.

We identified and unpacked her pattern of inaction. Angelica was capable; she was simply crippled by a false interpretation of the very natural interruptions storms can bring. Once we got to the root of the behavior, we replaced the binding belief system by first creating a list of the many things Angelica had accomplished. This list became evidence that Angelica was a capable woman who had a history of getting things done. You better believe we anchored her new narrative with a promise from the Scriptures she could quote whenever she was presented with a new storm or a new deadline. Her anchor passage became "My flesh and my heart may fail, but God is the strength of my heart and my portion forever" (Psalm 73:26).

Angelica launched her blog, by the way. I should also

mention her transformation took time and had many moments of relapse. But she pushed through them, and we count it all a success. If you can go to battle for your calling and your created self in the midst of a storm, that's success, honey. That's courage and confidence!

Forgiving Yourself

I have to be honest. There are some storms I've experienced that rolled up on me seemingly out of nowhere, and some that I saw in the forecast but proceeded on my way anyway. I put on my rain boots and walked right into the ensuing storm. Poor relationship choices I knew were not good for me. Bad spending habits and purchases I knew would gratify me at the moment but push me further into debt. I avoided going to church, like somehow God couldn't find me if I wasn't there. All because I was living a lifestyle that I wasn't ready to be confronted about yet.

Every decision I was making was leading me away from peace, away from my created self, and closer and closer to a storm. Each of those choices came with natural consequences, and I had to learn to forgive myself for being the one to bring them on. This is where we struggle the most. Making reconciliation with those bad situations we knowingly chose. The devil did not make me do it. I like to say, "He wasn't even in the country that day. I was doing bad all by myself."

In my first few years of ministry, every time I stood in a pulpit, I was convinced everyone could see my blunder-filled past.

I was positive they had my rap sheet, even the redacted parts, and they were holding it against me and didn't want to hear me preach or teach. What a lie. I was the one who was holding it against me, and it was time I forgave myself and moved on.

"It is finished" were the powerful final words of Jesus as He took His final breath on the cross (John 19:30). It became my daily mantra and weapon of mental warfare. I began to confront the enslaved thinking that kept me from fully standing in my created self by declaring, "It happened, and it is finished." Truth is, I was not damaged goods. I was a gem that survived a wreckage. Truth is, I was not a fraud. I had returned to my rightful position from a long hiatus.

It is time for you to forgive yourself, too, and change the narrative about your past. Right here, we are straightening your crown and realigning your purpose posture. Continuing to entertain inner and outer dialogues about who you are from the vantage point of the unfavorable places you have walked through will keep you tethered to the destructive patterns of your old experiences. It also creates a point of access for the enemy to slither his way back in and deceive you again and again. Forgiving yourself severs the umbilical cord. We are not feeding that version of ourselves anymore.

Would you permit me to speak further into your life?

I *declare* that your setbacks have set you up to be set forth in a greater measure of your purpose.

I *declare* that you have dominion over the place you presently occupy. You cannot lose.

Fear won't block your *purpose.*

Mistakes won't cancel your *purpose.*

Lack won't limit your *purpose.*

You walk in *confidence*!

You are *victorious*!

You are *blessed* to overflowing!

In Jesus' name, amen.

Add this to your wheelhouse of purpose clarity for the days you don't feel like the capable queen you really are.

The Benefits of Obedience and Surrender

Scarcity is described as shortage, lack, and want. Storing up all our "good feels" is so important to our survival during times of scarcity. I'd like us to address its impact on walking in the power of purpose clarity and why obedience and surrender have to be our highest good in times of need.

Every January, I begin the year with twenty-one days of prayer and fasting. After weeks of denying myself my favorite edible pleasures, I start to find things I normally would not eat appetizing. Casual drives past restaurants whose greasy menus I usually try to avoid fill my nostrils with sweet savory aromas. The number-one rule when ending this type of fast is to start light and not overeat. But it took a few years and a few episodes of intense stomach cramping to learn less is more when you've gone without.

The children of Israel also struggled with this principle. After their release from slavery in Egypt, their journey through the wilderness was met with a severe food shortage. God responded to their discontentment by providing bread and meat daily. That provision came with strict instructions to only take as much food as each person needed and to not keep any overnight. But how could they be sure this wasn't going to be the last meal before another long stretch without food? Why risk it? It would be a wise move to tuck a little aside. And that's what they did. In Exodus 16, some of the Israelites dismissed God's instructions and kept back some of the food until morning, but it was full of maggots and began to smell.

The challenge with periods of going without is that when provision does show up, whether it is food, money, invitations, opportunities, contracts, or a long-awaited partner, our fear of being without again can lead us to abandon God's instructions and find an alternate method of ensuring our needs are met.

A scarcity mindset says, "Get all you can, and can all you get." It pushes us out of trust and obedience concerning our business, career, love life, finances, ministry, and whatever else and into self-reliance. It also pulls us out of alignment with our created self, and we may even find ourselves compromising and making regrettable moves that carry crushing consequences. It is common to find ourselves, like the

Israelites, complaining and angry with God because obedience has led us to the point of shortage and lack we are currently experiencing. Purpose-led living requires you to see the bills piling up and still say no to that fifty-thousand-dollar contract because it conflicts with the instructions God has given you. It's tough. Survival mode can set in, and a scarcity mindset can take over. But we must be mindful that giving in to the same mindsets that the children of Israel gave in to will set us up for the same outcome—decay.

When a fighter is training before a match, she is either putting on weight or cutting weight. It seems logical that the bigger the fighter, the better the chances of winning. But it all depends on the fight. Lightweight fighters tend to be quicker and don't tire as quickly. Similarly, it may make no sense that your purpose-led walk has led you here. At God's word, you made a faith move and now you are experiencing lack—lack of energy, money, or _______ (you fill in the applicable shortage). This is your season to cut some weight. Maintaining your purpose posture will require you to fight the temptation to grasp at resources that God already knows are going to weigh you down. He knows what you are about to step into, and in the cutting, you are being prepared for acceleration and endurance.

> Let us not grow weary of doing good, for in due season we will reap, if we do not give up.
>
> GALATIANS 6:9

Reaping Your Fruit

I don't have a green thumb, but last summer I was introduced to chocolate habaneros, and as a foodie, it was a game changer. I bought four pepper plants and invested in a planter for my backyard. I researched and checked in with real gardeners to get the best advice on growing these peppers. Early each morning, in eager anticipation, I would go outside, wide-eyed, looking for any sign of peppers . . . and find nothing. I knew it would take time, but give me something! A little height on the plants, more leaves, something! One day I started to see flowers on one of the plants, but after a few streaks of hot days, they dried out. What a disappointment. My zeal for those early morning visits to the planter with my watering can waned. I soon forgot they were even there.

I have a few other things in my life where the zeal and passion have slowly leaked out. Flashes of my created self that I've seen with my spiritual eyes have been recorded in journals, but there is still no sign of fruition in my life. I've watered it, investing in education, professional development, and coaching. I've sought out mentorship, sat at the feet of people God told me to serve, and flown to another country in pursuit of nurturing it, but still no fruition. I've seen the vision produce flowers. But after a few stretches of thriving in my purpose posture, they seem to dry out.

This is not that feel-good chapter you may have been waiting on where I tell you that it's your time or that blessings are about to break forth in your life. This is the chapter where God grounds you and elevates your faith. There are some things that my heart aches to see come to fruition now, and I get tired of the wait. I've had days of remaining in bed when I told myself, *Not today*, but purpose kept nudging me forward. "When, God? When will You ________?" I'm still not sure how you will fill in the blank, but here is the one thing that I know: "I am sure of this, that he who started a good work in you will carry it on to completion until the day of Christ Jesus" (Philippians 1:6, CSB).

God cannot lie. Period. This is what I hold on to. I wrap myself up in its protection like it's a security blanket. God cannot lie. I remind myself of this grounding truth: Even if I am being wheeled out in my nineties or someone is shouting the headline to me at one hundred years old because my hearing is weak, there will be fruit.

And speaking of fruit. Remember those habaneros? After some time passed, I remembered I had not been to the planter in the backyard for a while. I was sure I was going to find those neglected pepper plants dead. When I arrived, they looked the same height and there were no . . . wait. One, two, three peppers hung there that I almost missed because they were the same shade of green as the leaves. Where the flowers had "dried up," peppers had sprouted.

It's the draining provocation of *When?* that retires many

purpose walkers prematurely. The wait can feel like a taunting no-man's-land where we're mocked for waiting on a bus to come when the last one pulled out hours ago. An unwatered *When?* will silently sap your joy, focus, and fruitfulness. So water your when. Give it a steady source of God's promises daily and sprinkle it with your words and actions. Continue to live and speak in a manner that is not weighted with the worry of *When?* but aligned with the promise of when.

I was so disappointed in how long my habaneros were taking to blossom that I almost missed those peppers. No, action is not the same thing as inaction in God's ecosystem of time. "Let us not grow weary of doing good, for in due season we will reap, if we do not give up" (Galatians 6:9).

There will be fruit.

Be Kind to Yourself

Maybe you haven't always been this diligent and purpose focused. Perhaps you've dropped several balls or started and stopped more times than you would like to count. But you are not counted out. Don't you think God knew about all your inconsistencies and blunders before He called you?

> [God said,] "Before I formed you in the womb
> I knew you,
> and before you were born I consecrated you;
> I appointed you a prophet to the nations."

Then I [the prophet Jeremiah] said, "Ah, Lord God! Behold, I do not know how to speak, for I am only a youth." But the Lord said to me,

"Do not say, 'I am only a youth';
for to all to whom I send you,
you shall go,
and whatever I command you,
you shall speak.
Do not be afraid of them,
for I am with you to deliver you,
declares the Lord."

JEREMIAH 1:5-8

When God speaks of "knowing" Jeremiah here, He is not referring to a casual awareness of his existence. The Hebrew word used is *yada*, which typically refers to a deeper level of knowledge ("understand," "perceive," "know by experience").[1] This insight is thorough. It is with this level of insight that God still chooses to call us to His purposes. But like Jeremiah, many of us respond to God with reasons why we cannot confidently say yes when He calls on us. Jeremiah responded with the two most common reasons we still hide behind today: an inadequate skill set and incorrect timing.

And there goes our Adamic gene kicking in again: the sin-curated reflex to hide when God calls on us. Adam and Eve used inadequate coverings from the trees of the Garden to cover their newly discovered nakedness. You and I use excuses to cover our own. Today we call our nakedness "vulnerabilities"—the parts of us that make us feel uncomfortable if seen. Has God ever presented you with an opportunity to use your gifts and you responded with "I'm not old enough" or "I'm too old"? Maybe you contended with God as though to bargain your way out of service by responding, "It's the wrong timing" or "It is too late. I've missed my time." God is the One who intricately knit you together while you were still a gas-like flutter in your mother's baby bump. Can you see now how comical it is when He calls and your response is "I don't have enough education, skills, or experience"? Imagine this not-so-funny image: every excuse hitting like the nails Jesus already bore in His hands and feet to ensure that you and I would forever be adequately covered. God simply needs your compliance, not your credentials. I dare you to just show up. Put the list of disqualifiers to the side, and show up.

The short version: In Jeremiah 1, God went on to tell Jeremiah all about his created self and instructed him to simply show up and that He, God, would ensure he was covered. So please be kind to yourself, knowing that God has made an informed choice and investment when He created you. As you face off with your curated self, you will win some rounds with ease and boldness. But, friend, for those rounds when God calls on you and you look at the task and then lie down and play dead, the act of showing kindness to yourself is the hand up you'll need in this private inner fight to get back up, choose your created self, and win.

I am a huge cheerleader for the underdog. I may let some cheap shots about me slide because as I get older, I don't have the energy for clapbacks or defending myself in every verbal attack. My skin has grown thicker, and my snapback from most things hurled at me has developed an impressive recoup time. But when I see someone who hasn't quite developed that same inner strength get verbally mauled, someone better hold my earrings and my purse. I'm a defender of those still finding their created self.

Can you picture it? All five feet and three inches of me flying across the parking lot to interject and come to a stranger's defense? Well, this is that moment. Hoop earrings off, designer purse on the curb—right here on these pages, I interject. I am compelled to interrupt that sabotaging narrative that has been robbing you of your destiny moments even as you read this chapter. I'm going to need you to cease and desist with the verbal and mental attacks on your own created self and be kind to yourself. You may have a trigger-ready list of things you cannot do, so before we proceed, why don't you take a minute to start a new list that reflects three attributes of your created self. I've given you a starter list on the next page. Spend some time in private reflection or ask a trusted friend for some help identifying three attributes you possess that prove you bear the image of God. Practice speaking to yourself and about yourself with the attributes from this list, and over time, you will find yourself autocorrecting instead of automatically canceling yourself.

innovative
trailblazing
creative
affectionate
kind
trendsetting
supportive
nurturing
comforting
giving
encouraging
advocating
peacekeeping
ingenious
analytical
resourceful
eclectic
dependable
governing

Celebrate Progress, Not Perfection

Perfection has never been a biblical prerequisite for obeying God's calling. It is the process that perfects us. I've held back so many profitable solutions and Kingdom contributions because I was waiting until I became more proficient or the pitch sounded just right. I never reached that point. I discovered that waiting doesn't alleviate our fears of failure; it feeds it. Wisdom is biblical, but we must be careful not to use our desire for the details as an excuse not to make moves. Walking in your purpose first starts with stumbling into purpose, wobbling in your purpose, and falling in your purpose. If ever anyone looks like they've nailed it, know that therapy, mentorship, coaching, and intercessory prayer probably preceded that.

Purpose can have the tendency to look effortless on others, but I would like to demystify that and take you behind the scenes. Discovering your purpose is one thing, but staying there is a whole other ball game. Some days you will move with ease, and other days it will feel like you've lost clarity. That is perfectly normal.

Celebrate your progress. Perhaps there was a time when you would have received negative words or disapproval and quit, but now you have a one-day pity party and move on. That's a win! If you used to need validation to feel confident enough to take action but now when someone disapproves of your ideas you may feel sick to your stomach yet take action anyway, that's a win! We can get so fixated on the person we desire to be and the milestones we want to achieve that we dismiss the important steps we had to take to get from point A to point B. So they passed the exam on the first try and you had to do it three times. You're still here. I have a learning disability that I have no problem talking about. I have to do things in a particular way to gain comprehension and retention. It can take me three hours to complete what is typically done in thirty minutes. Frustrating, yes, but possible.

Two fish and five loaves of bread. That is all Jesus needed to feed five thousand hungry men that day on the shores of the Sea of Galilee, not to mention the women and children who were not counted (John 6:1-14). The little boy whose lunch He used didn't need to have a culinary background, a food handler's certificate, or an industrial food warmer. What he had in his lunch that day was enough for Jesus to do what He needed to do. As you walk in your purpose each day, what you bring to the table that day is enough.

Chapter Check-In

It is time for you to forgive yourself and change the narrative about your past. Right here, we are straightening your crown and realigning your purpose posture. Continuing to entertain inner and outer dialogues about who you are from the vantage point of the unfavorable places you have walked through will keep you tethered to the destructive patterns of your old experiences. It also creates a point of access for the enemy to slither his way back in and deceive you again and again. Forgiving yourself severs the umbilical cord. We are not feeding that version of ourselves anymore.

Journal Prompt: I admit that I need to stop referring to myself as . . . I profess that I am . . .

Remember: You will have to guard against identifying yourself by the issues you are facing or have lived through. Where you are is not who you are.

5

The Box You've Overlooked

Unboxing Your Purpose

How often does it occur to us that
we are a gift from God to ourselves? . . .
Our life is a gift and a giving to others.

HANS URS VON BALTHASAR

Have you ever searched for your phone only to realize you were talking on your phone? I have more. Have you ever searched for glasses you were wearing, shoes you were carrying, or food you had already eaten? I really could do this all day. Similarly, many folks are on a quest for purpose in external places, when in reality our purpose has been with us the whole time.

We are hoping to find it in the right career choice or by picking the right ministry to serve in. Perhaps it's found in the right humanitarian cause or by determining which world problem we were created to solve. Purpose is not in any of those places. Those might be assignments we've been given, but they are not purpose. They might be great, God-honoring ways to use our gifts and natural abilities, but they are not our purpose. In fact, it is possible to be fully engaged in meaningful work and still miss the mark.

Jesus shared this sobering caution with his disciples about running the risk of confusing performativity with purpose: "Not everyone who says to me, 'Lord, Lord,' will enter the kingdom of heaven, but the one who does the will of my Father who is in heaven. On that day many will say to me, 'Lord, Lord, did we not prophesy in your name, and cast out demons in your name, and do many mighty works in your name?' And then will I declare to them, 'I never knew you; depart from me, you workers of lawlessness'" (Matthew 7:21-23).

What you are in search of has been within you this entire time. Purpose was never meant to be a mystery. God is not playing a twisted little game, finding amusement while we grope around in the dark trying to find purpose. In Ephesians 2:10, the apostle Paul exclaims, "We are his workmanship, created in Christ Jesus for good works, which God prepared beforehand, that we should walk in them."

The problem is, we are asking the wrong questions. Instead of asking, *What am I supposed to be doing?* Ask, *How do I bring who I am to the assignment in front of me?*

Inward clarity gives you outward clarity so you can make good, Spirit-led, purpose-informed choices. Romans 12 gives us the blueprint for discerning the will of God.

God's way of doing things is completely different from secular culture's. We can learn from secular culture, but we can't be led by it and expect to be able to perceive what God is doing. A quick social-media scroll can take our eyes from what God is doing in us and fix them on how someone else is getting things done. We should definitely pray about everything, but this is not what Romans 12 is highlighting. Our minds are in need of a constant rinse and repeat if we are going to be able to discern the will of God in new situations. When you get clear on the inside, things on the outside start to get clear too.

Purpose as a Lifestyle

The number one mindset shift you will ever have to make concerning your purpose is internalizing this:

> *Purpose is not a destination; it's a lifestyle.*
> *It is not a place you arrive to; it is a place*
> *you live from.*

This seemingly simplistic explanation of purpose is often hard for many to embrace. Let's clear up some language that we tend to use interchangeably to help us understand this further.

- **Purpose:** how we function

  The combination of our divinely given gifts, talents, temperament, and abilities that reflect the likeness of God.

- **Calling:** why we function

  An invitation from God, usually experienced as a strong, unwavering nudge to use our natural gifts, talents, temperament, and abilities in a way that serves God's plans and not our own.

- **Assignment:** when and where we function

  A divine directive or divinely ordered opportunity to use our natural gifts, talents, temperament, and abilities in a way that serves God's plans and not our own in order to be a solution to a specific place or group of people. It is intended to be executed within a set, discernable time frame. This may come with a set of specific deliverables.

Most of us have spent the better part of our lives searching for an understanding of what we were placed here on earth to do when the true pursuit is to experience revelation about who we are as God's own treasured handiwork. When we make this shift in our thinking, the question *What was I created to do?* becomes *Who was I created to be?* and then *How was I created to function?* How you function is your purpose. I get goose bumps just thinking about it.

Purpose Principles Found in the Bible

Here are some biblical examples of this purpose principle:

Joseph the Dreamer

Joseph was given the nickname Dreamer by his envious brothers (Genesis 37:19), who meant to use it as an insult but in actuality identified his divine gifting. At seventeen years of age, Joseph had his first recorded prophetic dream, and since no one around him wanted to believe it, they tried to bury it. Joseph was a leader, a good communicator, a natural problem solver, and a divinely gifted prophet. We don't see the breadth of Joseph's purpose until about a decade and a half later. Time and process meet calling and assignment, and he becomes the second-in-command to Pharaoh in Egypt. But at seventeen, Joseph was a boy living at home who was babied by his father, hated and bullied by his brothers, and a bit of an immature antagonist of his brothers.

Joseph's purpose was not attained when he became the governor of Egypt. That was one of his many assignments, the one that is typically elevated as the indicator that he had "found his purpose."

Joseph's calling was to use his divinely given natural abilities to help God's people gain an understanding of what God was doing in a particular time for His people. He yielded to that deep, unwavering nudge by living in his purpose, which was simply to function as the prophetic dreamer and leader that he already was. As we read about the life of Joseph in Genesis 37–47, we learn that he was constantly being chosen for leadership positions and growing in his prophetic gift as a dreamer-turned-dream-interpreter (and, additionally, as a wise strategist). From the time he was sold into slavery to his short stint in prison and then on to his appointment by Pharaoh to the palace as governor, no matter where life found him, life found him in his purpose.

PURPOSE POINT TO PONDER
Being in the right alignment will bring you to your right assignment.

Jesus the Savior

We are told in Matthew 1:21 at Jesus' divine conception that His name would be Jesus (which means "Savior") because He was going to "save his people from their sins." Jesus' calling was to point people back to the Father. As a result of His divine purpose and calling to save, help, rescue, deliver (the list goes on), we naturally find Him doing good everywhere He went, as we see throughout the New Testament. Specifically, we see Him functioning as Savior well before the

Cross. Jesus Christ had a uniquely climactic assignment: to die for our sins, making provision for our salvation. Thank you, Jesus!

But even Jesus' life story is filled with what I call "purpose pit stops." These are day-to-day moments where we encounter minor and major problems requiring a particular kind of purpose to solve them. (You guessed it: They require *our* purpose.) Jesus encountered the sick, the possessed, and even the dead. Wherever life found Him, life found Him in His purpose, functioning in His natural ability to heal, deliver, and even raise the dead. Even His detours turned into divine occasions for deliverance. Note this: As He functions as Savior, we also experience Him as Healer, Provider, Protector, and so much more. Like Christ, as we respond to life firm in the knowledge of Whose we are, more and more is revealed about who we are.

PURPOSE POINT TO PONDER
Taking action will reveal your function.

Paul the Apostle

Even in his pre-Damascus days, when the not-yet-apostle Paul was persecuting Christians instead of preaching to advance the spread of the gospel, he could have been said to be living his purpose. He functioned as a mouthpiece and someone on a mission, as is the loose definition of the word *apostle* (*apostolos* in Greek).[1] The difference from our previous examples is that even prior to Paul's conversion, we see his function at work. Paul is a strong leader, compelling communicator, and bold influencer. He was a Pharisee like his father, and his strong Jewish roots gave him an unparalleled zeal to honor his heritage and follow tradition. Tradition, however, can be an enemy to purpose.

Paul had the right functionality but responded to the traditions of his father instead of the calling of God, his heavenly Father. Purpose is as much *Whose* you are as it is *who* you are. Paul's "Who" gets a major realignment one day while he is on his way to approve the killings of more Christians. You can read about it in greater detail in Acts 9:3-9. Here is the quick recap.

Paul is surrounded by a bright light (confrontation). He falls down (conviction). God speaks to him (correction). Paul asks, "Who are you, Lord?" (confession). God answers (revelation). God gives Paul a new marching order (calling and assignment).

Paul's misalignment of his purpose with tradition had him on the wrong assignment for a long time. The worst part is that he was responsible for so much damage. The best part is that when Paul was confronted by God, he responded with humility to the conviction he was feeling and the correction he received. His humility positioned him to receive a greater revelation of Whose he was, and that revelation put him on track to the right assignment. Paul the apostle, as we know, went on to be a missionary and church planter who performed miracles by the working of Holy Spirit. He also wrote a significant portion of the New Testament books and was an integral player in outlining many of the foundations for Christian living.

PURPOSE POINT TO PONDER
Following tradition can lead you to an end God did not intend.

Let's delve into some more Bible verses to help you internalize this mindset shift. Making this shift will help you

- evolve in your purpose;
- trust the process of purpose;
- take more actions that align with your purpose;
- live daily in your purpose;
- find greater fulfillment in your purpose; and
- become more grounded in your purpose.

In Genesis 1 and 2, we find the creation story. Let's look specifically at the creation of Adam and Eve. In this account, we are made privy to a conversation God had with Himself (the Trinity) about His plans for creating humankind.

> Then God said, "Let us make mankind in our image [*tselem*], in our likeness [*demut*], so that they may rule over [animals]."
>
> GENESIS 1:26, NIV

This is so exciting and starts to put meat on our new mindset shift about purpose. The references to *image* and *likeness* are a type of Hebrew parallelism. The two words are almost synonyms for each other and really serve to emphasize—hear this—the intentionality with which we were made. You don't need a cause to plug into to have purpose.

When we skip ahead from the creation story to the account of the captivity of the Israelites in Egypt, we find a conversation between Moses and God that sounds a lot like the one we have with our self: *Who am I?*

> Then Moses said to God, "If I come to the people of Israel and say to them, 'The God of your fathers has sent me to you,' and they ask me, 'What is his name?' what shall I say to them?" God said to Moses, "I AM WHO I AM." And he said, "Say this to the people of Israel: 'I AM has sent me to you.'"
> EXODUS 3:13-14

We are the ones with the fixation on titles. We lead by what we do. It is where we tend to find our relevance and how culture decides who is valuable enough to be listened to or taken seriously. God has been known to go by many names, but the response "I AM" sent a message to both Pharaoh and Moses, that my existence is not dependent on what I do.

In the same way that God *is*, you are.

When I was in my teens, the office job of inbound telemarketer was the coveted job. I traveled miles, took tests, and aced interviews to get it. When I did, it was such a beautiful letdown. This is no disrespect to anyone currently in that role. This was true about most of the people and things I idolized at that time. Even if they weren't a beautiful letdown, once the mystery was gone, most things in life that I elevated started to look and feel like the Wizard of Oz—a little man with a megaphone.

Whether you are the CEO of Starbucks or a barista, you can show up as who you are, have impact, and still know you are walking in your purpose because it's not a destination; it's a lifestyle.

Seasons, Stages, and Iterations

Walking in this level of discernment and insight is not reserved for the church mothers or clergy. It's not even prophetic. It is practice. The more we exercise our hearing, sensing, feeling, reading, studying, and interpreting, the better we get at holding life's choices up to the Word—and God.

When God calls us, we experience an inward tugging toward an upward pulling. At this point, we are often unsure what is happening or what we should be doing, but we sense that God is trying to get our attention. For some, this is a feeling of uneasiness or discontent and, as a result, they may miss it. What you may be experiencing is a change in your assignment.

As the children of Israel journeyed through the wilderness, "the Lord went before them by day in a pillar of cloud to lead them along the way, and by night in a pillar of fire to give them light, that they might travel by day and by night. The pillar of cloud by day and the pillar of fire by night did not depart from before the people" (Exodus 13:21-22).

You must pay attention to when your cloud is moving and follow it. Purpose is who you are. As you serve the world with your gifts, never get attached to the location. This includes titles, jobs, and people or even your business niche, profession, or ministry. Living a purpose-led life requires fluidity because everything in life moves by seasons, with a set beginning and end. We can grow so attached to where we are that we overstay our visit long after the cloud has shifted, and we become exposed to the elements.

When I was in my traditional nine-to-five, an internal opportunity became available, and I expressed my interest in the position. A colleague of mine said, "Of course you are interested," and she pointed out a trend. She said, "You never stay in a position more than a year."

I had never realized that, but she was right. This made me feel like I had an inability to commit. Why couldn't I stay put? Why the discontentment after a year? Remember, I came from the generation that stayed. So why couldn't I stay put? Was I going to be able to succeed at marriage? I really thought I had a problem. I didn't know how to serve with longevity. But you will assess incorrectly when you don't know who you are.

I am a strategist and a launcher. I have a special gift for building and setting things in motion. I can see all the steps,

I mean all of them, like the character John Nash can in *A Beautiful Mind.* New excites me not because I get bored but because a different kind of power flows out of me in a particular stage of a project. I best served that organization with my gifts when things were new. I became the go-to for idea generation, even from people in programs and departments I had no experience with. New contracts were brought to me to be reviewed to implement strategy because people saw it came naturally to me. Senior leadership would seek me out to ask, "Nicole, if we got this extra $150,000 dollars, how can you see us using it?" I couldn't name it at the time, but there was something in me, and others could see what I only felt and had no clarity on. They saw an asset to project start-ups, and I called it being noncommittal.

There was a reason for the quick shifts in seasons. After several years of working in almost every frontline position within that department, I became the manager. Then it all made sense. Your seasons may not be as short-lived, but you will need to be able to shift when the time comes. What if I stayed because it was what I felt was required of me instead of what I sensed God was doing in me? Discernment didn't always feel like a God moment.

Practicing responsiveness to this type of discernment taught me how God communicates with me, and as you walk your own purpose journey, He will increase your capacity to do the same. I know it can feel scary. What if you make the wrong move? Lean into the character of God, knowing that a loving Father will not allow a misinformed act of obedience to wreck you but will always lovingly redirect you until you are where you need to be.

Not only do seasons change, but so do the expressions of your gifts. It is possible that after putting in the work to discover yourself and finally walking in it, you could find yourself back in a place of insecure questioning as God pulls out other parts of you and pushes those untrained, unexplored, uncomfortable parts to the frontline.

At the beginning of 2019, God told me, "You're going to preach more this year." I suppose it wasn't strange. After all, I am a minister. But . . . can you keep a secret? Even with four years of seminary and ten years of being a credentialed minister under my belt, preaching never really excited me. Teaching and training—now that was my sweet spot. I experienced the prophetic flow intensely when I taught. I felt like the world had enough preachers and congregations filled with people who didn't know what to do after they received the preaching. And I wanted to merge the worlds and teach people how to operationalize what they read in the Bible and integrate it into their daily lives. But true to His word, after three months of silence, the invitations to preach started to pour in.

What in the world? I thought. *I don't even want to preach.* Sure, I felt half-decent at it, but it felt weird and uncomfortable, and truly, I hadn't found my preaching voice yet. I always felt like I was stepping into a rendition of every preacher I had ever heard—*ick!* After day one of a three-day convention, I went back to my hotel room feeling horrible.

I had preached and led an altar call I tried to avoid, and the response was as mediocre as I felt. But night two, I was in my element. I led a workshop-style session, and the response was unanimous: "She's amazing!" I was booked for two more speaking opportunities by visiting pastors who, in their words, needed this kind of teaching for their team. The reviews were in, and I had done a great job.

I went back to my hotel room to settle a score with God. "See," I pointed out to God with arrogance, "I told you preaching isn't my thing. My teaching session is where my sweet spot is."

As I proceeded to inform God of all the obvious reasons I was right and He needed to stop pushing this preaching thing, He softly interjected. I was a trained facilitator with over twenty years of experience teaching and training groups. Of course it was a sweet spot and flowed with ease. He went on to explain that my preaching gift needed to be developed, and while I didn't feel as proficient in exercising it as I did in teaching and training, it was still a gift, and it was time to pull it to the front.

God continued to open both local and international doors that year, and something else started to happen. The prophetic flow I experienced during training sessions started to flow when I was preaching, too. I went from "I only pray for people when I feel led" to two-hour altar ministry and shutting down my sermon so I could lay hands on the people. What was I becoming? The world had enough of this, I reminded God. I am the one who teaches people what to do *after* the altar call. God lovingly responded, *Now I want you to do both.*

Purpose isn't one-dimensional. It has seasons where God will reassign you to new people and places of impact. It also has stages where God can take you from being the one who prefers being in the kitchen to the one leading the charge. And it has iterations, so don't be so quick to build real estate on the version of yourself you have grown acquainted with. Your forty-year posture might just be your prequel. So you don't do it like everyone else. A purpose-led life will often accentuate how different you are from your environment—and it's supposed to. Difference is not a fault; it is a gift, and the world is waiting for the unboxed, Creator's edition of you.

Realigning with Your Purpose

There is a temptation to pattern ourselves after the examples around us. It happens sometimes without us even trying. However, to tap into our place of brilliance and point of greatest impact, we must stay authentically aligned with who we are. I had a fall over ten winters ago that I never got treatment for. I slipped on a patch of ice and came crashing down with my full weight on my elbow and forearm jamming my shoulder. A heating pad and Advil, and I was off to work. Many years later I started experiencing pain all over my body. My left ankle was swelling, my lower back was aching, and the pain in my shoulder grew from mild discomfort to excruciating pain. Soon, I lost mobility of the same arm I had injured years ago, and the medical referral was to a chiropractor.

What did my back have to do with a swollen ankle and stiff shoulder? Our spine sits at the core of our body, and when it goes, the rest of the body will soon follow. Problems with our digestive system and all kinds of seemingly irrelevant ailments can manifest all because our center is out of alignment. I was out of alignment that whole time, causing a disruption in the rest of my body. A few pressure moves, and I heard a loud cracking of my spine. I got up from the chiropractor's table with full range of motion in my arm and shoulder blade. I'm talking backstroke and butterfly swim moves. As I left the chiropractor's office, God started to reveal the connection between the physical body and our spirit.

Life lands us all kinds of nasty falls, bumps, and bruises. A nasty remark we can't shake, a poor performance review that crippled our confidence, a debilitating health diagnosis, a marriage that ended, or that conversation between trusted friends you overheard that's tearing you to pieces.

You can time-stamp it. The day you fell or got the harsh jolt that shifted you from being confident and clear to indecisive and insecure. Many of these bumps and bruises go untreated as we rush back into performance and meeting the demands of our lives. Over time, this misalignment impacts our reach and mobility. It begins to cripple our drive, silence our voices, restrict our willingness to step up, say yes, and try new things. We find ourselves less impactful and more unhappy, and things seem to be slowing to a halt and breaking down. This is when God calls us in for a spiritual adjustment.

We must lie down before God and allow Him to put the pieces in their rightful places, snapping authenticity, gifts, talents, and temperament back into perfect alignment like the chiropractor did with my bones. That cracking sound was terrifying for a moment because it sounded like bones had been broken. Was I going to get up and discover I couldn't walk or that the right side of my body had now lost movement too? Jesus, the Great Physician, knows exactly what He is doing. And what sounds like your entire life breaking and falling apart is actually the sound of things falling into place. When you get up from time with God, your new purpose alignment has repositioned your purpose posture, and you are now ready to walk tall again.

I didn't just see my chiropractor that one time. I had to schedule maintenance visits because the body wants to naturally slip back out of place. Each month, I am required to get an adjustment and exercise to strengthen the muscles that surround my spine. Over time, I don't require as many intrusive treatments. As my muscles grow stronger, they help keep my spine in place for longer stretches of time. But every now and again, I must be laid out on the chiropractic table, heat is applied, the machine that relaxes tense muscles is required, and extra pressure must be applied for realignment to take place.

We need to stop assuming that hardship is God's response when we have done something wrong. Pressure is not God's way of punishing us. It is what He uses to posture and propel us. You are not being destroyed, my friend. You are being developed.

Your pressure is only momentary, and it has a mission. Find encouragement, and fix your focus on this:

> We are afflicted in every way, but not crushed;
> perplexed, but not driven to despair; persecuted,
> but not forsaken; struck down, but not destroyed.
> . . . So we do not lose heart. Though our outer self
> is wasting away, our inner self is being renewed
> day by day. For this light momentary affliction is
> preparing for us an eternal weight of glory beyond
> all comparison.
>
> 2 CORINTHIANS 4:8-9, 16-17

Staying in Your Lane

The resources we need and often look for to fulfill our assignments have already been prepared ahead of us, but we will only acquire them when we remain properly aligned with our created self, aka "stay in our lane." Consequently, life often feels the most intense when you are purposefully aligned with your created self. Pay attention to this because this is when you are most susceptible to satanic and self-sabotaging attempts to distract, derail, and detain you from your assignment and God's provisions to complete your assignment. This is because the enemy knows that your lane has enough God power to thwart the plans of the enemy and advance God's plans in the earth.

These sabotaging attempts don't have to be colossal to lure you away. For example, there you are, confident and clear. The news reaches you of someone getting married, having a baby, or celebrating a new achievement in record-breaking time, and you find yourself slowly being pulled out of alignment by comparison, envy, or feelings of insecurity and running for the shelter of your cowardly curated self. But don't you dare stay distracted and distressed. You can be shifted back into alignment with a prayer, worship, or a call to the right friend just as quickly as you shifted out of it. These are the moments you will have to contend for your freshly acquired clarity about who and Whose you are. You will have to become real schoolyard bossy and snatch your thoughts and emotions back so you can swiftly reclaim your posture and power.

If you give it some thought, you'll realize that a purpose-led woman like you already knows what will send her spiraling mentally and emotionally. If you continue to let those saboteurs pull you out of alignment with your created self, they will steer you away from the destiny encounters and Kingdom connections that God already intended for you to make along the way. These divine moments you prayed for will happen when you remain in alignment with your created self. Curating a version of who you are in order to operate according to someone else's pace or process will only defer or delay the people and places you were meant to be a blessing to and be blessed by.

A curated version of yourself will only land you in the wrong lane chasing someone else's assignment without the grace to complete it.

God provides grace for what He has graced. And that's you. Maybe you are not a lane hopper. Maybe instead you have settled into straddling lanes. One foot squared on your created identity and the other ankle-deep in people-pleasing and always locked and loaded with an escape plan. This non-committal place of ambiguity is where the grace that God extends us to be our created self is only experienced in small portions. It's a mere splattering, a light drizzle with chances of a shower compared to the concentrated outpour that we are positioned under when we are aligned with our created identity.

I was watering my plants one day and out of nowhere the water pressure lowered to a trickle. I thought that maybe my husband, who was at the other end of the connection, shut the water off before I was done. Once I followed the hose back to the pipe, I noticed that the water was still on, but as I had been moving about the yard the hose had gotten tangled and bent, impacting the water's flow.

As we move about life, we are prone to having our created self tangled and bent, like my hose. How we are positioned will mean the difference between access to a floodgates-of-heaven kind of power or a drought-like trickle, making the process of purpose harder and longer than God intended it to be.

When we come into alignment with our created self, we are positioned directly underneath God's outpour and covering. Wonder why it feels so heavy? This is the revelation I received from the Lord: "I have an anointing and a glory that's supposed to travel with you, but you're out of alignment. My anointing is falling on you. You are still experiencing opportunities and visions. You still feel that leap in your belly letting you know that purpose has not died, but you're walking with only a portion of what is available to you. You've gotten lost in the crowd, and it is weighing on you. I am calling for you to come out from among others. I recognize there is comfort in the familiar places you find yourself in, but your purpose and your oil are being compromised. You are persuaded by how everyone else is doing it, but there is another way. To you, it seems narrow and condensed, but for those who walk in it, it is deep, concentrated, and more than enough."

When you come into that kind of alignment, your wrestling is no longer over the destination you're supposed to arrive at in life and at what time you're supposed to get there. You become hyperfocused on who you are and how to maintain that level of clarity and conviction everywhere in your life. For the moment you begin to question and doubt the significance of your purpose and identity, you are questioning and doubting the significance of God.

What Is in Your Hand?

Within the composition of your purpose (who you are, not what you do), there are divine abilities you inherently carry. By "divine" I mean, even though there may be characteristics that you also see in your mother or the community that raised you, you have spiritual gifts that are given by the Spirit (1 Corinthians 12:4-9). You are not as ordinary as you feel. God has already hardwired you with the tools you need to be successful in this life.

One could argue that we don't need God since we have this hardwiring. But these are power tools, and while used on their own, one might get a bit of manual torque, they work so much better when plugged into the power source. We get to choose how we use our God-given tools. Many of us are manually pounding the pavement when if we just plugged into God's power, we would see that we've been sitting on a jackhammer the entire time.

Because attributes like temperament, talents, and spiritual gifts are such an intrinsic part of us, they often get overlooked or taken for granted. They become common because they have been with us our entire life.

The life of Moses and the deliverance of the children of Israel from Egypt are accounts I love reading again and again, because as a leader and coach who works from a purpose framework, they are such great depictions of purpose unboxed. The ten plagues aside, most people would mark the parting and crossing of the Red Sea the most memorable moment in the Exodus story. But there is another moment that captures my heart. It's when God appears to Moses in the burning bush and reveals to him that he possesses more than he realizes for the assignment ahead of him.

God asks what Moses has in his hand, and Moses replies, "A staff." It was common for Moses to have a staff. It held no significance aside from being a walking stick or a shepherd's staff. He carried it with him every day. But it was used in one of the first miracles Moses would see God perform. God tells him to throw it on the ground where it turns into a snake, and when he picks it back up, it returns to its common walking-stick form (Exodus 4:1-5). God is clearly with Moses. And after some time—you probably know the story—Pharaoh lets God's people go, and they are on their way to freedom and the land flowing with milk and honey. Can you picture it? If they were Pentecostals, I just know they would have been running laps. Moses must have felt amazing! God was with him; therefore, he could not fail. Yet not too long after their grand exit they meet their first opposition—the Red Sea.

Why does purpose seem to lead us to a dead end? With no way to cross the sea and Pharaoh and his army in hot pursuit to recapture the Israelites, the confetti soon turned to criticism of Moses' leadership. The people wanted to know what Moses planned to do.

The pressure was on, and not because Moses heard wrong at the burning bush or didn't have what it took to lead the people. This pressure was about to position and propel Moses into his assignment.

> The LORD said to Moses, "Why do you cry to me? Tell the people of Israel to go forward. Lift up your staff, and stretch out your hand over the sea and divide it, that the people of Israel may go through the sea on dry ground."
>
> EXODUS 14:15-16

Moses didn't have an escape strategy, but he did have something in his hand. It had been with him the entire time. Before Moses encountered God at the burning bush, it had only been used for herding sheep and for supporting himself. Since then, Moses had used his rod to perform miracles. On its own, it was just a staff. But it was still a tool for leading and walking—the two things that were needed in that moment at the Red Sea. God asked for action ("Tell the people of Israel to go forward") and implementation ("Lift up your staff").

What is in your hands? The assignment before you does not require a divine move of God. It requires a move from you to put your divine natural abilities into action.

Chapter Check-In

Most of us have spent the better part of our lives searching for an understanding of what we are placed here on earth to do when the true pursuit is to experience revelation about who we are as God's own treasured handiwork. When we make this shift in our thinking, the question *What was I created to do?* becomes *Who was I created to be?* and then *How was I created to function?* How you function is your purpose. Please don't underestimate that. So I ask you the question: How were you created to function? Write down your answers before a storm comes, causing you to forget.

Journal Prompt: My purpose can be identified in the ways I consistently shine and come alive when I . . .

Remember: Purpose isn't one-dimensional. It has seasons when God will reassign you to new people and places of impact.

6

The Box You Must Activate

Unboxing Your Power

God hath work to do in this world; and to desert it because of its difficulties and entanglements, is to cast off his authority. It is not enough that we be just, that we be righteous, and walk with God in holiness; but we must also serve our generation, as David did before he fell asleep. God hath a work to do; and not to help him is to oppose him.

JOHN OWEN

We have been empowered by Holy Spirit to serve our generation. The word *empowered*, however, has been watered down to a feeling. If we've been motivated we say, "I feel so empowered," but the word implies so much more. It means to actually hold power. The *Oxford English Dictionary* defines *empower* as to "give [someone] authority or power [to do something]."[1] The *Collins English Dictionary* defines it as "to give [someone] the means to achieve something."[2] Being an empowered woman of God means you have been given the authority and the power to achieve, attain, realize, accomplish, fulfill, and perform your Kingdom assignment. That endowment is way too significant to be reduced to an emotion that comes and goes with the entanglements of life.

Your created self recognizes this kind of power from the hands you were shaped by. Yet when you walk in your curated self, you forfeit that power every time you shrink, question yourself, or wait to be given permission to exercise the power you already have to impact your generation. Whether at home, on the job, in your business, or at church; whether great or starting out in small and humble beginnings, you have the means to perform your assignment. It's perfectly okay that at times you feel inadequate. That's what the power you have been given by Holy Spirit is for. You are not a damsel in distress waiting to be saved. You've been saved! If you are going to walk in the courage and confidence of your created self, you will have to start using the power you've been given.

> [Jesus said,] "Abide in me, and I in you. As the branch cannot bear fruit by itself, unless it abides in the vine, neither can you, unless you abide in me. I am the vine; you are the branches. Whoever abides

in me and I in him, he [or she] it is that bears much fruit, for apart from me you can do nothing."
JOHN 15:4-5

Activating Your Power

Life has a way of placing a demand on your gifts. A need presents itself, and unlike all the other times, this time, no one has stepped up to solve the problem because this time it has to be *you*. There you are, raising your hand, speaking up and stepping up in a way you have silenced or stuffed down before. You are activating the power God has given you. It was forced out of hiding like a little child whose mother is bellowing for them from the doorway in the middle of a round of hide-and-seek. You thought you had to be bold for it to work, but it is God's Spirit that gives you courage and confidence. When you speak in that boardroom, strategies come together. When others are stuck for ideas, you can't turn off your ideation mill. The average person is stuck for the right words to say in a crisis, but you rise to every high-pressure situation, knowing just what to do and say.

Let them call you quiet until you catch wind of injustice and you, my world-changer, cannot remain quietly indifferent. They don't even know your name, but hell sure does because when you pray, signs, miracles, and wonder follow. Even when you are aligned with your created self you will have moments of feeling petrified and paralyzed. But then power and purpose begin to pulsate like a homing device, and before you know it, you are operating at a level of efficacy, courage, and confidence that cannot be experienced without the power of Holy Spirit.

The *Cambridge Dictionary* defines the word *activate* in this way: "to cause something to start."[3] Plain and simple. Yet so many of the women I coach struggle to initiate or propel themselves into the areas they sense God calling them. God knows how to use the right set of circumstances to jump-start our created self.

Walking in the power of Holy Spirit doesn't require us to be perfect or to reach our misunderstood meaning of *ready*. Many people are discouraged from walking in the power that comes with being your created self because of the stumbling and fumbling that comes with newly operating in our God-given power. It makes us feel like we're doing it wrong. The good news is, the power is in the doing, not the delivery. The doing stirs up our faith, and our faith stirs God. God is the source of our power. We know this. I know we know this, but if we do not come back and unbox this foundational truth, over time we will find ourselves sitting on our power or turning to ungodly sources of power. We have one source, and when we begin to cross the wires with other sources of power, things in our life will start to short-circuit.

Who's Really in Charge?

If the question *Who is in charge?* appeared on a pop quiz for a group of Christian women, it would easily be answered with

"God." Yet how many of us *actually live* like we are convinced of this truth? As we unbox our ideas of power, I would like to take you through some popular biblical accounts of power from the life of Jesus.

After Jesus' resurrection, the disciples went to Galilee as He had instructed them to do (Matthew 28:10; Mark 16:7). Without fail, there He was, in all His resurrected glory. My own heart fills with awe and wonder as I imagine the happy reunion. The Scriptures tell us that they worshiped Him, but some were frightened and doubted it was Him (Matthew 28:17; Luke 24:37).

In John 2:19-22, we find Jesus in one of many conversations with the Jewish leaders. They wanted proof, a sign of His authority, and Jesus gave this as His sign: "Destroy this temple, and in three days I will raise it up." The Jews replied, "It has taken forty-six years to build this temple, and will you raise it up in three days?" But Jesus was speaking about His body. "When therefore he was raised from the dead, his disciples remembered that he had said this, and they believed the Scripture and the word that Jesus had spoken." Believe it or not, not all His disciples believed.

The disciples had seen Jesus' power firsthand while He was alive. Then there was all the teaching they received directly from Jesus Himself as they did life with Him daily. Not to mention the fact they had seen Him raise the dead multiple times. Yet when Jesus told them He would raise Himself up after three days, some of them doubted Him. Surely after all they had experienced and seen, they would never question whether Jesus had that kind of power . . . but they doubted.

The *Oxford English Dictionary* defines the word *authority* as "the power to give orders and enforce obedience."[4] If it really was Jesus who appeared to the disciples after His resurrection, it would mean He truly had the power to order death to let Him go and then to enforce hell's obedience. Those who doubted the authenticity of Jesus' appearance also doubted His authority. Many doubted that He had that kind of authority, but surely not His disciples. I'm pretty confident that none of them would have articulated their brief encounter with doubt as meaning they doubted Jesus' authority.

Jesus approached them and declared, "All authority in heaven and on earth has been given to me. Go therefore" (Matthew 28:18-19). In verses 19 and 20 Jesus outlines to the disciples their marching orders in what we now call the great commission. The disciples were being sent on a petrifying mission. Believing that it was Jesus standing before them was the first leap of faith to obeying His commission.

Something doesn't add up here. God's words + Scripture + more Word = doubt? Make it make sense! Now cue the personal introspection and conviction as I consider how many times I've had to be reminded of what God said concerning something He was going to do in my life, how I believed the related Scriptures and the word that Jesus spoke, and yet I still did not believe that something would happen. To doubt Jesus' words is to doubt His authority. For the disciples and you and me, doubting Jesus' authority would have a grave impact on what came next: the issuing and implementation of their assignment.

I am circling this doubt dialogue for an important reason. What we truly believe about God's authority impacts the ways we think, speak, and behave. You have had too much teaching and too many personal experiences and have seen God perform too many miracles not to believe that it is really Him calling you out of your fear, doubt, and comfort zone. I know what He told you to do seems impossible to pull off, but you are a woman who has been empowered by the One who has all power.

Jesus dropped a few verbal bombs on the disciples after appearing to them, took care of some other business, and then prepared to ascend back to heaven. But not before instructing them further. He shared,

> "I did not say these things to you from the beginning, because I was with you. But now I am going to him who sent me, and none of you asks me, 'Where are you going?' But because I have said these things to you, sorrow has filled your heart. Nevertheless, I tell you the truth: it is to your advantage that I go away, for if I do not go away, the Helper will not come to you. But if I go, I will send him to you. And when he comes, he will convict the world concerning sin and righteousness and judgment."
>
> JOHN 16:4-8

The fact is, Jesus came to save and Holy Spirit came to help. My heart sinks every time I read this account, as though I don't know where things are headed. I can't help but have the same guttural response: *So you're just going to up and leave?* Have you ever felt that way? It's like God just disturbed your entire existence with this tremendous call and assignment, and then you're left asking, *Where are you?* By ascending back to heaven, Jesus did not leave us neglected or alone. God sent another representative, in the person of Holy Spirit, who abides with us and gives us power as we navigate the rough places ahead.

As we continue the story, Acts 1:8 reads, "You will receive power when the Holy Spirit has come upon you, and you will be my witnesses in Jerusalem and in all Judea and Samaria, and to the end of the earth." Let's not overlook that the disciples were real people like you and me. Power or no power, they would have had relatable reactions, like "If He's not going, I'm not going" or "I never did much of the speaking or performed many of the miracles. Who's going to listen to me?" or "My Greek is questionable at best. There is no way I can learn so many languages." All their inadequacies were satisfied when Holy Spirit came upon them on the day of Pentecost in the upper room. This is the account of that day:

> When the day of Pentecost arrived, they were all
> together in one place. And suddenly there came
> from heaven a sound like a mighty rushing wind,
> and it filled the entire house where they were sitting.

> And divided tongues as of fire appeared to them and rested on each one of them. And they were all filled with the Holy Spirit and began to speak in other tongues as the Spirit gave them utterance.
>
> Now there were dwelling in Jerusalem Jews, devout men from every nation under heaven. And at this sound the multitude came together, and they were bewildered, because each one was hearing them speak in his own language. And they were amazed and astonished, saying, "Are not all these who are speaking Galileans? And how is it that we hear, each of us in his own native language? Parthians and Medes and Elamites and residents of Mesopotamia, Judea and Cappadocia, Pontus and Asia, Phrygia and Pamphylia, Egypt and the parts of Libya belonging to Cyrene, and visitors from Rome, both Jews and proselytes, Cretans and Arabians—we hear them telling in our own tongues the mighty works of God.
>
> ACTS 2:1-11

In an instant, none of the disciples' inadequacies mattered. No one needed special credentials, more education, or Rosetta Stone software to reach the world. Nothing is wrong with acquiring these along the way, but what you acquire is not the same thing as what is required to fulfill your assignment. The disciples had not even left the room before multitudes heard about the mighty works of God in their own languages—coming out of the disciples' mouths! As the disciples followed Jesus' instructions to wait in the room for the power of Holy Spirit, it might have appeared to those watching that they were in hiding after the Crucifixion. No one—not even the disciples—realized they were in the exact place they needed to be to be empowered to enact their assignment. You may have received instructions from God, personal or public, and now it seems like "everyone" is waiting to see what you will do with that prophecy, resignation, book idea, business start-up, or ministry announcement. As you take the time to unbox, it may look like and feel like you've reneged. No one—not even you—may realize that you are in the exact process you need to be in to activate the power you've been given to enact your assignment.

Are your thoughts, actions, and behaviors telling on you? If your beliefs about God's authority are still resulting in doubt, then this is a good place to further unbox with a simple prayer and confession from Mark 9:24.

Dear God, "I believe; help my unbelief!" Amen.

Renewing Your Power

I remember being in a prayer service as a little girl when my head started to throb. I had suffered from migraines since preschool, and that night, at about eight or ten years old, my faith was stirred. It was one of those "back in the day" services you often hear older folks talk about. The Spirit of God was moving, people were crying, and I wanted to experience what they were clearly enraptured by. God was in the room in a tangible way, and I wanted in. I went up to my pastor, who was ministering to someone through prayer, and he asked the group to quiet down so he could hear me. This moment seemed like grown-folk business, but I had a great enough need and enough courage to interrupt the happenings.

I was crying uncontrollably. My tears, which were fat and hot, clouded my vision. I could barely make out his face. Standing at a height of only four feet, I blurted out my request like it was bad food that didn't sit well in the stomach: "I want to be healed from my migraines!"

The adoration of the proud adults in the room grew to a loud cheer. But the pastor didn't join in. I will never forget his response. "If it's *your* migraine, then keep it," he snapped abruptly. His words all jumbled together in my mind like they were trying to become one. It was not the response you would expect a spiritual leader to give a child so clearly hungry for the things of the Spirit.

He went on to admonish—borderline rebuke—me for my use of the phrase *my migraines*. His reason being it had all the makings of unknowingly communicating that the migraine I wanted to be freed of belonged to me. That isn't true, though. Sickness doesn't belong to me. It was so simple it was almost embarrassing.

Now, don't read into it. Really, I'm fine. I have no childhood trauma resulting from that prayer-service experience. I chuckle now each time I remember it. My then-pastor might have been unsympathetic and brash, but I got the point. Sickness and anything else the enemy would ever throw my way are not mine to own. Even with my words. The experience helped align my faith, my speaking, and my spiritual posture in a way I needed going forward.

Lessons can sometimes be hard to learn, and as impactful as the one from that prayer service was, it was a lesson soon forgotten. Some thirty-plus years later, I was lying on my couch going on day five of a nauseating and crippling migraine. I closed the curtains and got out my cold compress to soothe "my migraine." Anyone who called and issued the standard greeting of "How are you?" was met with a faint response of "My migraines." As though to say "Fill in the blanks. You know how it is when I get one of *my* migraines."

After about the third call of the day, I felt an inward quickening. It was as if someone had abruptly snapped their fingers in my face to get my attention. I had done it again: taken ownership. I was claiming that migraine as mine, like a long-lost lunch container found on the last day of school before summer break. You know, the one that your mother told you not to come home without? I had done everything for those migraines except stand in my spiritual authority, align my words with good health, reject that spirit of infirmity, and claim the healing that was available to me according to the Bible.

Holy Spirit reminded me that as a daughter of God, I have access to the gift of healing. I didn't need to simply lie on my couch and nurse my condition like a powerless slave to sickness. I was in a unique position. As a daughter of God, I get to treat the symptoms (that's wisdom), address the source of the pain (that's wisdom), and drive out the spirit of infirmity (that's wisdom and authority in action right there!). I have been given power, and so have you.

Let me ask you: What crippling and debilitating issue have you created a custom label for, marked "This issue belongs to _____," inserted your name, and laid claim to? Have you forgotten, like I did that day on my couch, that you have been given power? Have you forgotten that you don't have to lie there and own the hell life sometimes hands you or whatever gruel it is serving on the menu for the day? Living a purpose-filled life will incite opposition of all kinds. Family conflicts, marital issues, a health hurdle, stress on the job, church hurt, financial strain . . . the list goes on. The good news is you have been empowered by Holy Spirit. Remaining in your created identity demands that you reset your created self to God's factory settings, again and again. In the words of Bible teacher Jackie Hill Perry, here is why: "The problem with our nature is that it corrupts our minds, inflates our ego, meddles with our vision, and darkens our understanding so that when God decides to tell us anything, we determine its integrity by how we feel over who God has revealed Himself to be."[5]

The first lesson to be learned as you unbox your power is that resetting is not regressing. It is how we submit to the regeneration of our mind and identity. Resetting is what winning in spiritual warfare looks like, not the weak posture it sometimes feels like. My laptop chooses the most inconvenient times to request a reset. "Wonderful! This is such a good time to reset!" . . . said no one ever. But this seemingly inconvenient rest happens when the computer discovers I am operating on an old or potentially harmful version of a program or system that requires an update. The reset allows the program updates to override the old with the new. Why? So that it can increase the efficiency of my device's performance and use of power.

Retraining Your Thoughts

I am often asked, "How do you stay motivated?" The honest answer is, I don't. Motivation is not my muse. There are days that my tank is low, discouragement sets in, and I am both physically and mentally depleted. At times like this, what is required is to choose rest over resigning from your assignment is staying clear about your mission, not motivation. I can never stress enough the importance of your thought life.

There isn't a day that passes that you will not be required to take misaligned thoughts hostage and make them bow down to truth. Some of those thoughts are spiritual attacks and others are an in-house job. We can be guilty of mentally abandoning opportunities before they ever have a chance of locating us. We are addressing a fundamental element of what it takes to make a purpose shift. Mindset is integral to how we shift and maintain our power.

There are two types of thought origins. The first type is

inherent thoughts that we form based on how we've interpreted the things we have lived with, around, and through; these thoughts are experiential. The second type is *inherited thoughts* that we knowingly or unknowingly live by and allow to inform how we see ourselves and the world around us; these thoughts are based on the legacy handed down to us. You can inherit stinking thinking, and you can also course correct those limiting internal narratives so they do not become real-life barriers. If you are going to interrupt unhealthy generational patterns and cycles, you must first interrupt them in your thinking. Romans gives us the pattern for interrupting and changing those thoughts:

> Do not be conformed to this world, but be
> transformed by the renewal of your mind, that by
> testing you may discern what is the will of God,
> what is good and acceptable and perfect.
> ROMANS 12:2

Have you ever stopped to do an audit of your thought life? Have you ever wondered why some people seem so optimistic and full of faith, while others seem to walk around with a dusty, pessimistic, faithless attitude toward life? Our thought life becomes our lived life. And while simply thinking differently is not enough, it is certainly the launch pad of our purpose trajectory. As we pull and rein in our thoughts, we create the kind of tension required to catapult us into God's purposes.

Psychologists at Queen's University in Kingston, Canada, released a study that suggests we have 6,200 thoughts a day, on average.[6] That's a potential of 6,200 votes daily in favor of what empowers you or 6,200 votes in agreement with what enslaves you (or some combination of the two). A shift to purpose-led living needs to be positively and biblically reinforced daily, and we are physiologically rigged to enhance it. That's approximately

6,200 opportunities a day,
43,400 opportunities a week,
173,600 opportunities a month,
2,083,200 opportunities a year.

The gravity is jarring, but the odds are in your favor. Your life will produce from its roots. If you can shift it at its roots, you can produce a new kind of fruit. It's time to bring your season of purpose into fruition. That's power. You have been empowered to work with Holy Spirit to shift it.

If you have spent most of your life coming into agreement with your fears and insecurities, plus you have unhealthy, inherited thought patterns about money, marriage, trust, men, travel, church life, or (insert your dialogue here), then shifting it will take some work, but it is possible.

I discovered at some point in my thirties that I had been swallowing incorrectly my whole life. Try it. Swallow, and note which direction your tongue moves in. A proper swallow involves your tongue rising to meet the roof of your mouth and then sliding backward into the swallow. It's a wonder I ever kept food in my mouth all these years because I swallowed forward in what is known as a tongue thrust. This "condition" was slowly pushing my teeth forward and causing an overbite. Not too tragic, right? I paid over $3,000 for orthodontic work to align my teeth, but my habit had to be corrected, or it would constantly undo the hard and painful work that three years of wearing braces had done to enhance my smile. The solution: a tongue trainer. Oh yes, there is such a thing. A two-headed, spiked piece of hardware was installed at the back of my upper front teeth so that every time my tongue would move forward, it would be met with a subtle prick from the spikes. It wasn't enough to simply tell me to swallow backward. I had spent thirty-plus years swallowing in a particular direction. My tongue needed to be trained to move in a new direction so that my new smile wouldn't be compromised.

Your power shift requires the same kind of preservation, a retraining of your thought life so that the work you are putting into walking in your created self is not compromised by old patterns of thinking. Here are four ways you can renew your mind daily and train your brain to think more like your created self.

1. **Use visual prompts.** These are messages you leave for yourself in visible places. I have used sticky notes on my monitor, writings on my bathroom mirror, and even a T-shirt with the message I need reinforced.

2. **Set mindset reminders.** My coaching clients have raved about this one. Set a calendar event with the title of the message you are training your mind to think about. Set it as a daily or weekly recurrence. There is something amazing about having your day interrupted by a timely, personal, and encouraging message.

3. **Use biblically based affirmations.** There are two approaches to this one. Either (1) search for Bible verses that align with your mind training or (2) use Bible verses that have already left you feeling like God was speaking to you directly. Personalize them by including *I* or *mine* where applicable. You can even insert your name for emphasis.

   Here's an example of one of my own based on Jeremiah 1:7-8:

   > But the Lord said to me, "Nicole, do not say, 'I am too young.' You must go to everyone I send you to and say whatever I command you. Nicole, do not be afraid of them, for I am with you and will rescue you," declares the Lord.

   Challenge yourself to memorize as many of these affirmations as you can. Recite them, pray them, use them as declarations, and Holy Spirit will bring them to your remembrance at just the right time.

4. **Get an accountability partner.** This could be a friend in your current circle or a coach or therapist. The goal

is to share your mindset goal with someone you interact with regularly enough that they can lovingly call out your slipups. You'd be surprised how many times in the first fifteen minutes of a coaching session I catch new clients creating an atmosphere full of words that are negative, unbiblical, and unproductive.

Perhaps you've already done the mind work or the perspectives you've inherited are healthy and sound, yet you are not producing good fruit (actions and behaviors) even though your thoughts are rooted in good ground. This is what I call purpose unplugged, when what we know (in principle) is not what we know (in praxis). This is the crux of the apostle James's words here:

> What good is it, my brothers, if someone says he has faith but does not have **works**? Can that faith save him? If a brother or sister is poorly clothed and lacking in daily food, and one of you says to them, "Go in peace, be warmed and filled," without giving them the things needed for the body, what good is that? So also faith by itself, if it does not have **works**, is dead.
>
> But someone will say, "You have faith and I have **works**." Show me your faith apart from your **works**, and I will show you my faith by my **works**. You believe that God is one; you do well. Even the demons believe—and shudder! Do you want

> to be shown, you foolish person, that faith apart from **works** is useless? Was not Abraham our father justified by **works** when he offered up his son Isaac on the altar? You see that faith was active along with his **works**, and *faith was completed by his* **works**; and the Scripture was fulfilled that says, "Abraham believed God, and it was counted to him as righteousness"—and he was called a friend of God. You see that a person is justified by **works** and not by faith alone. And in the same way was not also Rahab the prostitute justified by **works** when she received the messengers and sent them out by another way? For as the body apart from the spirit is dead, so also faith apart from **works** is dead.
>
> JAMES 2:14-26, EMPHASIS ADDED

Intentional action is both an agent of true transformation and the proof of it. Faith must trickle down to our feet. What we know must cause us to go and take action.

Certain types of security boxes use a two-key verification process. Both keys must be used in order to open and shut the box. Even if the content inside the box is yours, you are still required to have both keys to open it. You could have been the one who registered for the safe. You still need both keys to gain access. Have you been wrestling with a locked door in your life? Some areas that just won't budge or that you feel powerless against, no matter how much faith talk you throw at them? Faith without works is dead, or to hyperbolize the point, faith without works is a dead bolt. You have been empowered with both keys. Go use them, and unbox your power.

Chapter Check-In

Life has a way of placing a demand on your gifts. A need presents itself, and unlike all the other times, this time no one has stepped up to solve the problem because this time it has to be *you*. What need has presented and re-presented itself, but you are still uncertain if you're the one to meet it? This is your sign. You are the one!

Journal Prompt: Three ways I will own my power differently are . . .

Remember: Being an empowered woman of God means you have been given the authority and the power to achieve, attain, realize, accomplish, fulfill, and perform your Kingdom assignment.

7

The Unboxed Woman

Principles for Maintaining a Confident and Purpose-Filled Life

When you walk for Jesus an entire life, it is a challenge . . . because trials will hit you all the time, and there are temptations to distrust God. . . . It's a fight, and this battle has got to go all twelve rounds.

RANDY SMITH

I was in school when I watched the movie *The Great Debaters*, which was directed by Denzel Washington. It is the story of a teacher at a predominantly Black college in the 1930s. He decided to start a debate team, which was socially unconventional for the deep South during that time. It also featured an even more unheard-of anomaly: a female debater. If you have never seen the movie, I apologize for the spoiler. I am about to completely ruin it for you as I jump forward to the movie's climactic end.

Jurnee Smollett, who plays the female debater Samantha Booke, steps up to the podium in front of a mostly white audience of her peers and adults. She cradles her fair-skinned, brown hands, one in the other, which have turned red from where she has been picking at them from sheer nervousness. Samantha had been in the room for every debate leading up to the one that day. She knew her argument inside out and had committed her speaking points to memory. She had all the signs of a confident communicator, yet that morning her Sunday bests made a slow and delayed heel-toe, heel-toe clicking sound as she timidly made her way to the podium. You just knew she was unsure, intimidated, and afraid. While I'm sure it wasn't the intended highlight of the movie, what rolled off her trembling lips is the most impactful single word that I've heard to this day. It is used several other times in the movie, but in this scene, on her lips, that word has never left me, and that word is *resolved.*

Resolved is the word every great debater uses before their grand speech. Samantha's delivery was ironically low and timid and lacked the conviction that the opening argument is meant to communicate. Stick with me. This will all prove beneficial. As she delivered her well-formed argument, several people in the audience got up and started walking out from under the event tent. Samantha cleared her throat and began again, this time with slightly more volume and a growing confidence. Even more people started to exit, as though lunch had just been announced in another room. The longer she continued speaking the more her delivery and conviction intensified because her message was not only political but also deeply personal. As Samantha's focus became less and less on her foes and friends, her confidence soon matched her convictions: *Be it resolved.* Seeing the faces of her opponents, the hostile audience, and her supportive teammates no longer mattered. She was focused, on mission, and resolved.[1]

A Redeemed Resolution

The use of the statement or introduction *Be it resolved* or *Resolved* is from *Robert's Rules of Order*, America's foremost go-to on parliamentary procedure.[2] Most boards, organizations, and professional associations use this guide for governance and decision making as well as presenting issues for debate. The profundity of this common word *resolved* led me to do some digging. I had to turn to the highest authority for information and research: Google University. My search for an explanation of the phrase yielded this explanation of its use: "Our reasoning is such that our position is the only logical one." The question or issue being debated is framed as a resolution rather than as an issue to be argued over or that has to be proven to be true.

Resolved. I had been brought to this kind of conviction before. I felt so strongly about Jurnee's convincing performance because I had come across that kind of personal resolution before in my devotional time. In Romans 8, the apostle Paul writes about the hope you and I, the daughters of God, can find in the face of our present suffering and weaknesses. My suffering was nothing like Paul's, but I bore my own kind of suffering—the kind I think you can relate to as well.

I have been right where you are, unsure of myself and questioning every little decision. That kind of inward battle is torturous. You are full and then empty, confident and then a cowardly lion. The inconstancy robs you of time, opportunities, peace, and most importantly, obedience to Jesus Christ. Then Paul writes his own resolution: "I am convinced that neither death, nor life, nor angels, nor principalities, nor things present, nor things to come, nor powers, nor height, nor depth, nor any other created thing, will be able to separate us from the love of God, which is in Christ Jesus our Lord" (Romans 8:38-39, NASB 1995). Resolved.

Unboxed and Unwavering

Samantha's experience in that scene from *The Great Debaters* is a great example of what you can expect as you begin to unbox for the first time—courage and confidence. Showing up as yourself even when the environment is hostile does not require the absence of fear. As you practice unboxing and become reacquainted with your created self, you'll have plenty of moments of making big moves but still feeling like you are small. I use the word *practice* intentionally because unboxing is both a practice and a discipline. Expect people to exit your life as you resolve to be your created self. Not everyone will be comfortable sharing space with your created identity. In all fairness, if you have been curating parts of your identity to fit in or appease others, the shift will have some blowback. It will inspire some and insult others. When this happens, don't shrink; instead, take up more space.

The sight of yourself might even frighten you at first, but as you occupy the places your gifts make room for, you will naturally grow in confidence. As you grow comfortable in holding your own, being your created self will no longer be an abstract concept but will become a deep conviction. Then you will find yourself looking less and less to others for permission and the assurance that your purpose-led moves are the right moves for you and that you have actually heard the voice of Holy Spirit. Resolved.

You have spent a considerable amount of time unboxing. Finishing this book is not the end of the process. For some of you, there are conversations you need to have, emails that need to be sent, places that need to be left, relationships and experiences that need to be worked out with a therapist, and thoughts and beliefs that will require further retraining. Please don't let life distract you from putting in the work. If you've read this far, then you are almost there. I can feel it. Have faith that even as you turned the pages, completed the challenges, asked yourself some hard questions, and prayed along with me, God was answering.

Abandoning everything you've curated is scary. It may leave you feeling vulnerable and unsure, but don't look back. Please don't curate new cover-ups. Your created self is breathtaking and exactly what we all need right now. Fight for her with the tools you've learned in this book. You will find, with time, the frequency of the battles will lessen as you work and serve as your created self. To unleash and maintain your created self is no small feat. Celebrate yourself. It's the one thing we all don't do enough of. You may not have the resources to buy some flowers or take yourself to dinner, and that's okay. All I am asking you to do is stop and acknowledge whatever amount of unboxing you've done—because progress is progress. What does your unboxed self look like? If you remember I started chapter 1 with a picture of an unboxed woman. I would like you to go back and review that if needed and then meet me back here to write your own vision of your unboxed created self.

Let me help you with a journal prompt to get started. You can recognize a woman who has been unboxed. This kind of woman is . . .

Unlike Beyoncé, we do not simply wake up like this. This kind of woman is high-maintenance and requires intentional disciplines to keep her from slipping and sliding too far from her created self. Her heart and mind must be guarded.

Proverbs 4:23 says, "Keep your heart with all vigilance, for from it flow the springs of life." You need to identify and memorize your identity resolutions so they are on hand when you need to remind yourself of who you are. It is also one of the ways I check in with myself when I am feeling a conversation, interaction, or opportunity pulling me out of alignment with my created self. I use my own resolutions to fact-check decisions and opportunities by asking, *Does this align with what I know about my created self?*

I have turned down phenomenal, paid opportunities to speak because they did not align with my created identity. I was also able to pass those opportunities on to other women whose resolutions were so clear it showed in their work and how they show up in life, and I automatically knew they would be a better fit.

How about you? As you unbox what have you learned or confirmed about yourself, what do you need a strong resolve not to bend or break? If you are already aware of these resolutions, please write them down in your journal to reference until you know them by rote. Like I always say, "Write down clarity when you have clarity." If you haven't already identified your own, here are three resolutions every unboxed woman should have to maintain her created self.

1. Resolved: I Know Who I Am

You need a clear vision of who you are. Remember: Where you are is not who you are. When I speak of "who," I am always referring to your created state and not your curated state of being. You need to be able to look at yourself and have the spiritual discernment to see yourself as you are, especially when you are pressured to perform or become something that is not aligned with your purpose. As you unbox, you will find that your created self just needed some polishing and dusting off. I love the way the *Oxford English Dictionary* defines *vision*: "the ability to think about the future with imagination or wisdom."[3] I am drawn to the word *wisdom*. Wisdom is the application of the knowledge you have. As you acquire fresh revelation about yourself, you must apply that knowledge to your attitudes, behaviors, actions, and thought life.

Vision is what you run by. It is how you operate, how you decipher your next move. It is a map by which you navigate life. Your vision should be operational, not a stagnant ideal. Knowing who you are requires the kind of vision that has foresight and insight. You need to be aware of who you are and the movement of Holy Spirit as He starts to expand your vision with fresh thoughts and capabilities that were always there but never awakened. Who you are is evolving as He smooths out rough edges and sharpens dulled gifts.

It was a vision that led the three magi to Jesus, and it was a vision that provided Habakkuk with a way of escape. When you have this kind of resolve you date differently, dress differently, and steward your time differently. It informs what you do, instead of what you do informing who you are. What you do becomes a natural overflow of who you are without all the wavering.

2. Resolved: I Will Take the Next Step

Do you want to know how to make wise choices that are aligned with who you are? Write this down somewhere: "Clarity gives you the ability to choose wisely." As someone who wears glasses, I am acquainted with squinting. Are you? Or have you seen it? Some poor souls like me lean in to see more clearly or have to rely on the vision of those around them to make out what they can't see.

If your next steps were etched on a billboard a far way off and you could not make them out, standing around and squinting at them for an extended period of time would not help you see them more clearly. You are then left with two options: Rely on the vision of those around you, or move from where you are to get closer. The choice seems obvious; however, fear and insecurities keep many of us stuck in the same place, relying on those we think are smarter, more successful, or more spiritual to tell us what they see. Here's what I need you to do: Take a step. With all your worries about not making the right choice, start to move in the direction of what God is calling you to. That may look like following the divine nudge to call someone even though you're not sure what to say and having them say, "I was just in need of prayer, and I didn't know who to call."

Perhaps it looks like making a call to a sister-friend and sharing your heart about a gathering you've been wanting to have for women, and she offers to cater for free. It could also blow your mind further by you applying for a job you have no business applying for only to discover the hiring manager pulled your résumé because she recognized your name from the time you unknowingly blessed her, and she had been praying for help in her new position. I didn't have to make any of those up. I've made calls to people only to have them answer the phone weeping and in need of prayer for their child. I had a vision about an event for women, and I had never hosted an event before. I didn't know where to start. I made a few calls, shared my heart, and found a network of women willing to help me pull it off. That event has grown into a global annual event with over one hundred and fifty women in attendance. I knew it was time to leave my job, but I wasn't receiving callbacks from any of the places I applied to. I followed a nudge even though the position didn't feel like what I was looking for, and the hiring manager turned out to be a woman I had given a gift to more than ten years earlier. I had felt led to bless her with an item I had just received. It was beautiful, and the tag was still on it when Holy Spirit prompted me to give it away. She shared over our phone interview that she had been going through a difficult divorce at the time, and that item had made her feel beautiful again and special. She never forgot the gesture and remembered my name. She also went on to share that she had been praying for help for a new role she was in. It was both a role and a program I had years of experience managing. Look at the ways God continues to move when we respond with action to the ways in which He prompts us to move.

With every timid step you take you get closer and closer, and your vision becomes clearer, and clarity gives you the ability to choose. Uncertainty is not an indication that you should sit tight. Making a move is how you get clearer. Even if that clarity is to sit tight. Either way, you have just moved from unsure to *I'm sure*. Take small steps. They count too. Not every move has to be the kinds of big leaps that are popularized on social media. The more you practice moving, the better you'll get at discerning if it is Holy Spirit telling you to move.

You have an assignment you've been sitting on, and now that you've unboxed, it's time to move. Using what God gave you is an exciting space to occupy, but you must guard wisely. You can guard something without being guarded. Guarding your gifts does not require you to be cryptic and shrewd. It simply means using common sense about who, how, where, why, and when your gifts are offered. As Jesus said, "Do not give dogs what is holy, and do not throw your pearls before pigs, lest they trample them underfoot and turn to attack you" (Matthew 7:6). Not everyone deserves a seat at your table. At this level of resolve, accessibility to your abilities is not always granted.

Know who you share with. Let time reveal people's character and intentions. Watch for godly character, consistency, and the fruit of the Spirit. Where you serve is wherever you are planted, but you are not required to put all your gifts on the table. Burnout is real, so pace yourself and set healthy boundaries. That may involve setting boundaries for yourself and explaining them to others when necessary. As a wife, mother of four, pastor, and coach, I am the go-to person for many people. Nothing brings me more joy than when my gifts of prophecy, administration, or knowledge are engaged. It brings me joy and a great sense of accomplishment when the gifts and abilities God has given me help others solve a problem or take action on their assignment. But what about Nicole? My health, my peace, and my time? I guard my gifts by knowing when to say no. My resolutions are not in place just so I can take action. They also help me know when I should avoid taking action. I keep my phone on silent and take calls when it is convenient. I have set times for checking and responding to emails and texts.

Knowing who you are is valuable. So valuable you ought to guard it. The HALT method is used for those in recovery from an addiction, but I have been practicing it for years and sharing it with my clients. While your gifts are spiritual, your body is temporal. I learned the hard way that your gifts don't work if you don't work. HALT is a handy acronym and reminder to take the time to check in with ourselves for self-care and self-awareness. It promotes that we should never allow ourselves to get too **h**ungry, **a**ngry, **l**onely, or **t**ired. After working with hundreds of women, I hold to the conclusion that in many instances we are not out of ideas, we are simply tired; we are not in distress, we are just hungry. I can't tell you how many crises have been averted by having a bite to eat, unboxing our feelings, getting in community, or taking a power nap. Taking responsibility for what is within our control will help us live more purpose-filled lives.

3. Resolved: I Know Whose I Am

A huge weight is lifted off your shoulders when you know Whose you are. I am totally team faith and works, but within all your doing there must be room for the divine. Some of you are wired to do it all. You've been nurtured into an unhealthy modality of being the one you depend on to get things done. But we've unboxed that already, and I implore you to not turn back. There is religion, and then there is relationship. If you have been reading and you are familiar with Christianity but not with Christ, I would like to take this opportunity to lead you out of religion and into a relationship with Jesus Christ. Religion says, "I believe there's a God." Relationship says, "He is my God." Religion invites God into special moments. Relationship walks with God daily in all the moments. Which perspective is yours? If you have never made a personal commitment to living with and for Jesus Christ or if you have walked away from your relationship with Jesus but remained religious, I would like to invite you into a relationship with Jesus right now by leading you in this simple prayer. If you are already a daughter, then pray along too. I love moments like these when I get to renew my commitment. Whether yours is an old relationship that needs rekindling or one that is brand new, Jesus is here in this ordinary and unconventional moment, waiting just for you. Pray this with me now.

Dear God, I know You are real, and it has always been my desire to know You more intimately. Please forgive me for thinking it was enough to profess being a Christian without living it out completely. Thank You for sacrificing Your Son, Jesus Christ, for my sins. I commit my life fully to You now and invite You to be Lord over every area of my life. Thank You for receiving me as Your daughter, and I look forward to this new, intimate chapter in my life as Your child. In Jesus' name, amen.

This Is Bigger than You

I have taken many faith moves over the years. I've just shared three of them with you. It would be easy for me to take the praise and say "Look what I've done" or "Look what God has done for me" because of my actions. But it's all bigger than me. When you start to live a purpose-led life as your created self, you will reap many benefits . . . but darling, the ripples cannot be counted. Showing up in the world as your created self gives others an invitation to do the same. Your actions have reactions that ripple through the earth and the heavens. There are souls who said yes to Jesus from watching your life, and you will never know about it. There are women you'll never be aware of who will learn, eat, be inspired, take action, increase in faith, pay their rent, leave a bad situation, stop abusing a substance, stand up for themselves, or step into a new opportunity all because who you are flowed over into what you do and a simple everyday task had a ripple effect.

Walking in your purpose is bigger than you, and God would never leave the responsibility solely on your shoulders. Not only is He in you to give you power, but He is also with you to provide you with grace. If you are going to be able to go the distance, then you must learn how to lean into and depend on Jesus. You must see Him as the owner and yourself as the caretaker of your gifts. There is no better feeling than knowing I did my best, even when my best feels like it was not enough and that God will not withhold His hand from me. You cannot manipulate God's hand to move by how much you work. God moves when you do what He's asked you to do. Do you want to know a little secret? Even when we fall short of meeting His expectations, there is grace and forgiveness for our shortcomings. Here's some more good news: That looming feeling of doom, like you are missing a purpose mark that you can't find? We've unboxed that, too, and I would like to remind you that purpose is not a place you get to; it's a place you live from, and that place is your created self.

Your Gift Is God's Investment

Know this: "We have this treasure in jars of clay, to show that the surpassing power belongs to God and not to us" (2 Corinthians 4:7).

God chose you. You can list as many shortcomings as you would like, but He still chose you. Simple you with super gifts?

It makes no sense in our social hierarchy. People travel the world to get a glimpse of some of the world's most beautiful wonders. My husband and I traveled to New Brunswick from Ontario and saw the most splendid sight. We didn't even know it existed. There we were at Bay of Fundy, where the tide gets so low that you can walk on the ocean floor. The actual ocean floor! There we stood, where the water had previously been over forty-five feet high. Have I mentioned that I only stand five feet three inches tall? I was completely awestruck. I considered how science calls this "low tide," but I knew the hand of God was holding the waters back. Soon, where my feet had recently stood on dry land, I was covered up to my thighs, and my husband had to pull me in. I also thought about the children of Israel, and then I could understand how completely possible it was for them to cross over on dry land and then have their enemies swallowed up by the water moments later. Second Corinthians made so much more sense. When we find treasures, God's treasures, in unlikely places, we see glimpses of His surpassing power and know that there must be a God. Don't giggle, but whenever I travel, the moment I get to swim out deep into the ocean, I start crying and singing the old hymn "How Great Thou Art."

Do you have any giggle-worthy moments when you become flabbergasted by the vastness of God? Just think about it. The fact that something as extravagant as the image and likeness of God can be found in something as simple as you and me. When you unbox, brush aside the debris, and reclaim your created identity, the world gets a glimpse of your Father.

> [Jesus said,] "Let your light shine before men in such a way that they may see your good works, and glorify your Father who is in heaven."
>
> MATTHEW 5:16, NASB 1995

It is not prideful or boastful to shine in a way that brings attention to you. Depending on your temperament, how you were raised, or how you were churched, you may really struggle with this one, but it's right there in black and white. Hiding is not humble. Playing small serves no one. Who you are should start to bring attention to Whose you are so others will glorify your Father, who is in heaven. If you have a tendency to hide, here is a modified list of Lolly Daskal's "13 Confident Ways to Overcome Your Shyness."[4]

Don't tell. No need to make an announcement about your tendency to hide.

Avoid the label. Don't label yourself as shy. Just be you.

Stop self-sabotaging. Don't let your inner critic win.

Know your strengths. Make a list of all your positive qualities.

Choose relationships carefully. Give time to those who get you.

Avoid bullies. Yes, adults face them too. Keep these people at a distance.

Remember that one bad moment doesn't make a bad day. Avoid overthinking. It probably isn't as big of a deal as you think.

Shut out your imagination. You may feel rejection that is not there. More people are for you than you think.
Stare it down. Face fear head-on and then do what you need to do.
Name it. List all your jitters and worries and make a plan to eliminate them.

After all the unboxing you've done, we're not going to let anything interfere or hold you back.

God Wants All of You

I have been there. On the fence with one foot in and one foot out. When God nudged me to leave a job I'd loved for over ten years, I moved with a quickness. When He opened the door for me to leave the traditional workforce, I walked right through it and built my own Christian coaching firm. I was in new and frightening territory. I fell in love with my new work—my own work. And after several years of toiling, I was finally outearning my previous salary, had found my niche, and was making an impact. Then it happened. The nudge. God wanted me to make a new pivot, and I was slightly mad at Him. So I double-dipped and had my hand in the new area He was calling me to while keeping a grip on the thing He asked me to leave alone. I could sense it wasn't one of those farewell situations—it was more of a "not right now"—but I loved it, and quite frankly, I needed the income, so I held on to it.

You can probably guess what happened next. The old thing started to dry up. My flow of new clients became a trickle, and things that were always fruitful were yielding no results. The new thing, the God thing, was hard to get off the ground. Relationships felt strenuous, and it felt like I couldn't produce the productivity I was known for in the new place. It took me longer than it should have, but I finally figured out what the problem was. God wanted all of me. My lack of trust was not only impacting my work for God, it was also impacting my relationship with God and my relationship with myself. I felt divided, drained, and unhappy. I also felt compromised and conflicted all the time, and neither space felt purposeful. God allowed my circumstances to make the decision for me. It became as though my old thing was slowly pushing me out. I had to let go. Not only physically but inwardly. My heart was occupied with things that no longer aligned with God. He had moved and sold the apartment, and I was squatting there.

Staying aligned with your created self will require you to let go of your old apartment. It represents the place you and God shared some great experiences, but He is no longer there. You've unboxed your relationships, but is your heart still there, haunting the memories of what was? When God closed that door, did you stick your foot out to catch it and leave it partially ajar? Take some time in quiet reflection and ask Holy Spirit to show you the doors of your heart that need to be closed.

Resolved: It All Ends in Victory

We fear letting go completely because we also have a fear of losing. The thing is that in God's economy one plus one equals zero. He is after the singularity of heart. Much of this is a review, but you need the reminder because old habits die hard. The encouraging outcome is, you don't lose when you try and "fail." As you practice His presence, you are perfecting your discernment. As I get older, I realize more and more that nothing is wasted. From the jobs I thought were insignificant to the relationships that left me devastated. Everything worked out for my good and my growth. From the events I launched that no one attended to the monies I've loaned that were never returned, nothing was wasted. As I serve God from this unboxed place, this woman is stronger and smarter for all of it. While I don't believe in reincarnation, I've had so many experiences that sometimes I feel like I've lived many lives. I have learned that what I have lived through are many lessons.

We win. Let that fuel you after you have unboxed and discovered that being your created self leads you into some difficult experiences. You win. May that anchor you when going back under the covers feels more natural and easier. *I win*. Let that be your resolution when you experience rejection after rejection because in the end, it all ends in victory for those who are in Christ Jesus (Romans 8:28).

Dying to your curated self may feel like self-betrayal after identifying with that version of yourself for so long. As you hold your ground and familiarize yourself with who you were created to be, you may feel like you are living with a stranger. The work that you've put into unboxing may be interrupted by life, responsibilities, and bad news after bad news, but in the end, you win. This may feel like gloom more than like good news, but as I told you at the beginning of this book, I love you too much to lie to you. There are gifts locked up inside you that God is trying to get out of you, and the enemy will throw as many darts at you as he can to keep this from happening—but "ha ha," you win! I am willing to forfeit a feel-good ending if it means that you will have the insight necessary to dodge the darts, take a few hits, and bounce back up because you already know that it all ends in victory.

Chapter Check-Out

Here's some grown-woman commentary for the road. It will require guts and grit to live a purpose-led life. There will be joyous moments. Many, many joyous moments. But there will also be some wounds. It's the way of the warrior, and as long as you remain in your created self, you win. Continue to unbox as you go. It will give you a greater perspective, increase your joy, and allow the mind of Christ to dwell in you richly.

Remember: You cannot stay where you are any longer. Not one more day. Your true home—the version of yourself that has been divinely inspired and wired—cannot be filled by anyone but you. You have not missed your chance. And even though many of the things declared about you seem delayed, they are still yours for the taking if you are ready and willing to make a courageous move toward the life of purpose you were *created* for.

Nicole xo

Acknowledgments

To God—Thank you for entrusting me with this mission. Thank you for holding my hand through every painful-yet-necessary season of unboxing in my own life. I am forever grateful for every door you swung open and for those you closed in order to bring this book to fruition. Thank you for not passing this assignment on to someone else during all those years you were gently knocking and asking, "Where's the book?" Lol. I hope this makes you a proud poppa and that it makes you smile.

Evon—My purpose partner, covering, friend, and priest. May God bless you for every prayer, foot rub, and hand massage. Thank you for keeping the kids in check because, as you would say, "Nicole's working on her bestselling book!" There was never a late night of writing without you curled up on the couch sleeping because you didn't want to leave me alone. My apologies for the intrusive light from my laptop and iPhone whenever a download of writing would hit, often at 2:00 a.m. This book could not have been birthed without you. I love you, Smitty.

Pops (Makih), Nahshon, Ahli (Ahliana), and Ethan—You all deserve a prize. Thank you for all the meals you ate in silence so I could concentrate on writing. Who does that?! Thank you for checking in on days I never left my room. Thank you for your understanding when my need to focus meant you all had to go without or do a little more. Thank you for celebrating every milestone like I was a superstar and for believing this book would help millions of women even though I'm still not sure you know what it's about, lol. Love you guys!

My squad: Nicole, Cheryl, Tammie, Michelle, and Denise—You are the manifestation of the kind of support network I prayed for. You pushed this book across the finish line when I had nothing left to give. Thank you for being the number-one hype squad in the world. You covered me with your prayers and celebrated for me when impostor syndrome wanted to rob me of owning this accomplishment. Thank you for the night you all refused to go to bed until I messaged the group chat "Finished" and submitted my completed manuscript! Thank you for being the hands, eyes, and ears that helped spur my own unboxing journey over the years and for nourishing me throughout this process.

My family—Melvin and (late) Shirley Salmon, thank you for doing your utmost with what you had to steward your baby girl and her gifts. Thank you for giving me room to be creative. You instilled in me the courage and confidence to refuse to play small and to believe that I can be anything and everything God shaped me to be. To my big brother, Shawn, thank you for your protection. Your quiet strength and admiration have never gone unnoticed.

Pastor Colvin and Monique Chambers—I remember us all, Pastor Kadeem included, standing at the altar with my publishing offer in hand. Thank you for praying over and throughout this process. Your check-ins, counsel, and listening ears are truly appreciated.

Embolden Media Group—Thank you to my agent, Jevon Bolden, whom I affectionately call "Pastor Jevon." It is a rare gift in this lifetime to come across someone who believes in your vision just as much as (and at times even more than) you do. You are that gift. Your mentorship, council, coaching, and advocacy have been a tremendous blessing. May you be rewarded richly on earth and in heaven.

Kia Stephens—You are this generation's hidden treasure. Without knowing it, you renew my faith in Christian sisterhood daily. Thank you for giving so generously, and I am thankful for every door God used you to open. Thank you for sponsoring me by calling my name in rooms I didn't even know I needed to be in. Congratulations again on the release of your first book baby, *Overcoming Father Wounds*. Your leadership and advocacy for Christian women of color who are called to write/speak is truly inspiring.

Church of God in Ontario—How could I not pay homage to my spiritual roots? Thank you to this faithful denomination and to its leaders for their investment in my gifts.

Thank you for providing a strong biblical foundation and for being a village through my most formative years.

NavPress—Thank you for honoring and trusting my voice as a writer. My biggest fear was that this wouldn't happen. You ensured that I had a first-class-citizen experience as a Black woman in an underrepresented sector. Thank you to my amazing acquisition and development editors, along with the amazing NavPress team and partners at Tyndale House. I feel seen, I feel heard, and because of your investment, lives will be transformed, including my own. Thank you.

Beyond the Book Media—Thank you for your amazing writers' community. Your boot camp was where I learned how to write the gold that is a book outline. This dedicated, prophetic space is where I spent the early phase of this book-writing experience, penning chapter after chapter under your covering and mentorship. Thank you for your vision to create this much-needed resource.

My community—To everyone who, without knowing it, was the voice of one crying in my wilderness, thank you. Your seemingly random texts, DMs, and Instagram-feed comments are some of the many ways God used to inspire, confirm, and affirm me along the way. Thank you for your prayers. Thank you for responding to requests for feedback, reading early excerpts, and offering your talents to edit if needed. Thank you to those who dropped Starbucks and meals at my door because you knew I was neck-deep in edits. Some of you fed my family, too, because you knew I had not even showered much less cooked in two days. Lol.

Whatever it was that you did, thank you. There are way too many of you to name, but you know who you are, and I pray the blessings of the Lord overtake you and that He rewards you openly for every private act of kindness you have shown.

Notes

CHAPTER 1 | THE NEED TO UNBOX

1. Daniel Nevers, "A Brief History of Hiding in Plain Sight," in *In Plain Sight*. Oakland, CA: Mills College Art Museum, 2019. Exhibition catalog, https://mcam.mills.edu/publications/inplainsight/nevers/index.html.
2. In AMP, bracketed text was added for clarity. These words are not present in the original text.

CHAPTER 2 | THE BOX YOU WERE GIVEN

1. Blue Letter Bible, "Lexicon: Strong's G4995—*sōphronismos*," accessed June 2, 2023, https://www.blueletterbible.org/lexicon/g4995/esv/mgnt/0-1.

CHAPTER 3 | THE BOX YOU'VE OUTGROWN

1. Personal communication to author, January 30, 2023.
2. See, for example, Cinthia Benitez, Kristen P. Howard, and Jennifer S. Cheavens, "The Effect of Validation and Invalidation on Positive and Negative Affective Experiences," *Journal of Positive Psychology* 17, no. 1 (2022): 46–58, https://doi.org/10.1080/17439760.2020.1832243; and Danielle J. Brick et al., "Celebrate Good Times: How Celebrations Increase Perceived Social Support," *Journal of Public Policy & Marketing* 42, no. 2 (2022): 115–132, https://doi.org/10.1177/07439156221145696.
3. *Merriam-Webster*, s.v. "codependency [*n*.]," accessed May 10, 2023, https://www.merriam-webster.com/dictionary/codependency.
4. Conversation with author, January 30, 2023.

CHAPTER 4 | THE BOX YOU'VE CURATED

1. Blue Letter Bible, "Lexicon: Strong's H3045—*yāḏa'*, " accessed May 11, 2023, https://www.blueletterbible.org/lexicon/h3045/esv/wlc/0-1.

CHAPTER 5 | THE BOX YOU'VE OVERLOOKED

1. Blue Letter Bible, "Lexicon: Strong's G652—*apostolos*," accessed May 12, 2023, https://www.blueletterbible.org/lexicon/g652/esv/tr/0-1.

CHAPTER 6 | THE BOX YOU MUST ACTIVATE

1. *Oxford English Dictionary*, 4th rev. ed. (2006), s.v. "empower [*v.*]."
2. *Collins English Dictionary*, s.v. "empower [*v.*]," accessed May 16, 2023, https://www.collinsdictionary.com/us/dictionary/english/empower.
3. *Cambridge Dictionary*, s.v. "activate [*v.*]," accessed May 16, 2023, https://dictionary.cambridge.org/us/dictionary/english/activate.
4. *Oxford English Dictionary*, 4th rev. ed. (2006), s.v. "authority [*n.*]."
5. Jackie Hill Perry, *Holier Than Thou: How God's Holiness Helps Us Trust Him* (Nashville: B & H Publishing, 2021), 50.
6. Julie Tseng and Jordan Poppenk, "Brain Meta-state Transitions Demarcate Thoughts Across Task Contexts Exposing the Mention Noise of Trait Neuroticism," *Nature Communications* 11, 3480 (2020), https://doi.org/10.1038/s41467-020-17255-9.

CHAPTER 7 | THE UNBOXED WOMAN

1. *The Great Debaters* (Chicago: Harpo Films, 2007). Based on a true story.
2. Henry M. Robert III et al., *Robert's Rules of Order: Newly Revised*, 12th ed. (New York: Public Affairs, 2020). Originally published in 1876.
3. *Oxford English Dictionary*, 4th rev. ed. (2006), s.v. "vision [*n.*]."
4. Lolly Daskal, "13 Confident Ways to Overcome Your Shyness," Inc.com, June 15, 2015, https://www.inc.com/lolly-daskal/13-confident-ways-to-overcome-your-shyness.html.